GW00498505

The MONOCLE
Travel Guide Series

Los Angeles

For more information,
please visit *gestalten.com*
————
Bibliographic information
published by the Deutsche
Nationalbibliothek: The Deutsche
Nationalbibliothek lists this publication in the Deutsche National-
bibliografie; detailed bibliographic
data are available online
at *dnb.d-nb.de*

Monocle editor in chief:
Tyler Brûlé
Monocle editor: *Andrew Tuck*
Books editor: *Joe Pickard*
Guide editor: *Ed Stocker*
————
Designed by *Monocle*
Proofreading by *Monocle*
Typeset in *Plantin & Helvetica*
————
Printed by *Offsetdruckerei
Grammlich, Pliezhausen*

Made in Germany

Published by *Gestalten*, Berlin 2016
ISBN 978-3-89955-680-3

© Die Gestalten Verlag GmbH &
Co. KG, Berlin 2016

Welcome
—— La La Land

Summing up Los Angeles in a few words can be tricky due to the multiple personalities it displays and conveys. The eastern part of the city – the hills, the views, that up-and-coming sense of change – seems to have little in common with the communities pegged to the *Pacific coastline*. Indeed at one point that disparity was seen as LA's downside: it felt more like a series of neighbourhoods and districts than a coherent city.

All that is changing, however, as public transport increases, Downtown continues its resurgence and residents realise that there's a wide world out there to be explored. Forget the *Hollywood bubble* (although we really wouldn't mind a house up in "the Hills", it has to be said) and explore the infinite options that the metropolis has to offer. You won't be short of ideas or options – in fact you'll probably have to narrow your field if you're going to achieve everything, especially given the sprawl and the traffic. Yet despite the bad rep the city sometimes gets for its smog and congestion, it's also almost impossible not to *fall in love*.

It's a city that swallows you whole and feels a million miles away from its east coast rival New York: LA is constantly sunny, *perennially laidback* and enjoys an enviable location, sandwiched between mountain and ocean. It's easy to see why it lures creative talent from across the US and travellers in droves. Welcome to LA. — (M)

Contents
—— Navigating the city

Use the key below to help navigate the guide section by section.

 Hotels

 Food and drink

 Retail

 Things we'd buy

 Essays

 Culture

D Design and architecture

S Sport and fitness

W Walks

Map
—— The city at a glance

Los Angeles is a sprawling city. It sits on a hilly coastal plain bounded by the foothills of the Santa Monica Mountains to the north, the San Gabriel Mountains to the east and the Pacific Ocean to the southwest.

With more than 100 neighbourhoods it's not an easy city to pin down but this map illustrates the key places you should get to grips with. Each area has its own personality and stories to tell – whether it's star-studded Beverly Hills or sporty Venice, a cultural hub such as the Arts District or museum-packed Exposition Park.

This guide will help you discover your own favourite spot; it's time to explore.

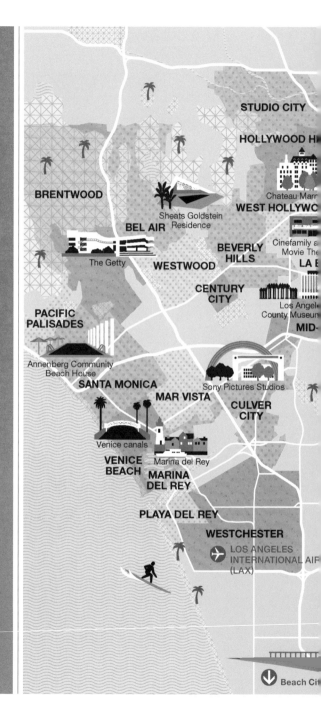

STUDIO CITY

HOLLYWOOD H

Chateau Marr

WEST HOLLYWC

BRENTWOOD

Sheats Goldstein Residence

BEL AIR

Cinefamily a
Movie The

BEVERLY HILLS

LA E

The Getty

WESTWOOD

CENTURY CITY

Los Angel
County Museun

PACIFIC PALISADES

MID-

Annenberg Community Beach House

SANTA MONICA

Sony Pictures Studios

MAR VISTA

CULVER CITY

Venice canals

VENICE BEACH

Marina del Rey

MARINA DEL REY

PLAYA DEL REY

WESTCHESTER

LOS ANGELES INTERNATIONAL AIR (LAX)

Beach Cit

Need to know
—— Get to grips with the basics

Navigating your way around LA – both physically and socially – requires a strategic approach. Here are some tips to help you plan, whether you're trying to avoid the notorious traffic jams or attempting to organise a rendezvous with an Angeleno.

Get your honk on
Traffic

Nowhere is driving quite so common – and quite so celebrated – as in the City of Angels. Be prepared to see valet parking galore, but not a lot of pavement life (except in some select neighbourhoods; – see our Walks chapter).

Make sure you plan when you get in the car. In theory, rush-hour times on weekdays are 06.00 to 10.00 and 15.00 to 19.00 (on Friday afternoon it's busy from 14.00 until 21.00). Weekend traffic is unpredictable, but an early start during the day and avoiding the 101 North to Hollywood on a Saturday night is always wise. In reality a traffic jam can appear at any time, so keep calm and have a good soundtrack to ease the pain.

In LA you're never far from a camera and that includes while driving. With red-light cameras throughout the city, the risk of having your picture taken when committing a traffic violation is highly likely. However, there is a light (that's not red) at the end of the tunnel – you can avoid paying the $300 fine because it's not always enforced.

While it's true that the car is king, the city is embracing new modes of transport. You can take advantage of LA's cycle lanes and bike-share programmes; the Metro, once a joke to locals and visitors alike, is now a stress-free option (you can get from the mountains to the beach for less than it would cost by car and without the headache); and as for walking in LA, it might sound alien, but it's more common than you think.

Taking sides
Neighbourhoods

Describing where you're staying in the city is a lot easier when the places are all designated with such catchy names as K-town (Koreatown) and The Hills (the ones in Hollywood). Where you stay will dictate what you do during your visit (given the traffic and distance).

The city is divided by the 405 freeway. The west is the place for those seeking a laidback, beach-friendly vibe, where you're that much closer to the Pacific and road trips up and down PCH (that's the Pacific Coast Highway; stay with us). The east side of the freeway, while not as polished as Santa Monica, makes up for it with creativity, history and charm.

Global village
Demographics

Los Angeles is a joyous, bracing blend of different demographics: nearly half of its 3.8m residents are Latino and there are sizeable African-American and Asian populations – including the largest Korean community of any city in the US.

What? My wings are tired. It's a big city

Going downtown
Urban revival

A mix of anonymous skyscrapers and art deco-style theatres long past their 1920s glory days, LA's Downtown was, until quite recently, an unprepossessing neighbourhood and a ghost town after office hours. But over the past 10 or so years, it's undergone a transformation, combining flagship art and performance venues, notably the Walt Disney Concert Hall, a lively restaurant and bar scene and some smart hotels. Whether this urban revival can lay the foundations for a sustainable community – rising rents are a problem for the creatives who make Downtown such an appealing destination – remains to be seen but it's still well worth a visit.

Rules of engagement
Social planning

Angelenos are very uptight about making plans; if you're looking to have dinner or get together for drinks, a minimum of three days' notice is required. Travel logistics alone need two. Anything less, unless you're around the corner, is pushing your luck.

Mo' money
Payment

Nothing gets the coffee guy's heart pounding like a bit of cold hard cash casually stuffed into his tip jar. So whether you're showing thanks for your Moon Juice Brain-Tonic or trying to get into that new club, it is cash, not card, that'll get you a taste of the high life.

Hat? Check.
Backpack?
Check.
Map?
Uh oh...

Green scenes
Parks

It's infamous for its pollution but this city has far greener pastures than you might think. At every point of the compass, you'll find trek-worthy landscapes that offer lovely views: well-known options include Runyon Canyon and Griffith parks, but for a less-trodden escape try Kenneth Hahn State Recreation Area or Elysian Park.

Keep an eye out for snake holes – although snakebites themselves aren't common, stepping into a snake hole and spraining your ankle is.

Life's a beach
Where to lay your towel

You're in California – one of the global heartlands for beach culture – so if you want to get under the skin of this mystifying city then you're going to have to spend some time on the sand.

Venice Beach is the eccentric aunt of the bunch: while some decry the number of tourists, it's still home to a freewheeling community of soapbox poets, palm readers, pavement musicians and rollerskating seniors in lamé bikinis.

Malibu is more understated than you might expect given its pop-culture notoriety and the number of celebrities who call it home, while Santa Monica's pier is throttled with tourists and souvenir shops and should be avoided. The Southern Beaches (Hermosa in particular) are low-key and increasingly hip.

There's a reason why wetsuits are ubiquitous: the water is cold year-round (the average temperature is a bracing 16C).

Who says
I need a
wetsuit?

LA without a map
Safe travels

LA is a sprawling, vastly populous, almost unmanageably large conurbation, and like other global cities of similar stature some areas will appeal more to the curious visitor than others. Exploring the city without decent planning can be disorientating and can land you in unending strips of featureless suburbia or areas blighted by the effects of crime and social deprivation (Downtown's Skid Row should be avoided). We recommend you follow the lead of this guide: it will give you a full sense of the real LA without any of the trouble or risk of its less salubrious quarters, and we promise there's enough here to hold your attention – not just for a single visit but many more.

Hotels
—— Homes away
from home

From honeymooning
silver-screen icons and
gambling gangsters to
rockstars riding the halls
on motorbikes, LA's
hotels have long been
playgrounds for the city's
highflyers – and they've
got the stories of scandal
and intrigue to tell for it.
    As you'd expect, they
also cater to every taste
and geographical desire.
You may choose to base
yourself in the bustle of
Koreatown – not far from
the centre – or opt for
Downtown, a place that
continues to evolve and
refresh itself. Then there
is the classic, old-world
glamour of Beverly Hills
and Bel-Air to consider.
    Wherever you end up,
you're sure to find rooftop
bars, swimming pools
and world-class
amenities aplenty.
This is LA after all.

Sunset Tower Hotel, Hollywood
The high life

Built in 1931 as a luxury apartment
block, the Sunset Tower was once
home to notable residents such as
Frank Sinatra, Howard Hughes,
Marilyn Monroe and Jean Harlow.
    The building underwent a
$46m renovation in the late 1980s
(reinstating some of the art deco
elements), and again in 2005 under
new owner Jeff Klein. While the 81
rooms occasionally feel in need of
another refresh, the old-school
charm is a rare pleasure. Staff
are attentive and courteous, the
poolside with its city views is an
oasis, and the Tower Bar (*see page
46*) is one of the best places to grab
a drink in Los Angeles.
*8358 Sunset Boulevard, 90069
+1 323 654 7100
sunsettowerhotel.com*

MONOCLE COMMENT: Mobster
Bugsy Siegel was kicked out of the
Sunset Tower for running an illegal
gambling ring from his apartment,
now the famed Tower Bar.

②
Hotel Bel-Air, Bel-Air
Serene scene

This 103-room hotel is set high in the hills and feels far away from everything (including phone service, occasionally). Though in truth it's less than a kilometre from Sunset Boulevard, the surrounds – nearly five hectares featuring 3,500 plants and trees – make it an utterly serene retreat. The hotel has been a hideaway since opening in 1946.

Many of the suites offer beautiful canyon views and there are private garden patios and wood-burning fireplaces set to a backdrop of limestone floors and wooden ceilings. The La Prairie Spa, tucked within the pale pink stucco property, should not be overlooked either.
701 Stone Canyon Road, 90077
+1 310 472 1211
dorchestercollection.com

MONOCLE COMMENT: Despite having a lengthy roster of high-profile guests, dating back as far as Princess Grace of Monaco in the 1950s, Hotel Bel-Air's bar is still a hangout for LA residents. Its black-and-white photographs were taken by neighbour and patron Norman Seeff.

Of course we can go for another walk down Rodeo Drive, Fifi

③
The Line, Koreatown
Classic K-Town

Occupying a restored modernist
block in the beating heart of
K-town, The Line's eclectic design
cues, buzzy nightlife and diverse
food offerings are a true reflection
of the neighbourhood it calls home.
Inside are rooms that all boast
floor-to-ceiling views; brushed
concrete walls are offset by Mexican
fabrics and commissioned artworks
that add colour and liveliness. Its
two restaurants and café are a
collaboration with famed street-food
chef Roy Choi and span a broad
spectrum of LA's culinary scene,
while an international newsstand,
well-equipped gym and rooftop
pool leave you with little to want.
3515 Wilshire Boulevard, 90010
+1 213 381 7411
thelinehotel.com

MONOCLE COMMENT: Beloved
boutique retailer Poketo has looked
after the in-house concept shop,
so leave space in your suitcase for
a few choice knick-knacks.

*A lounger,
a bottle of
pop and 'The
Monocle Daily'
on the radio.
Heaven*

Pools

01 Beverly Wilshire, Beverly
Hills: This European-
inspired setting mimics
Sophia Loren's private
pool in Italy and the
building itself was used as
an air-raid shelter during
the Second World War
(adding to the old-world
feel). A spa treatment
gets you a day by the
pool here and staff
will also provide Evian
spritzes if the city heat
gets too much.
*fourseasons.com/
beverlywilshire*

02 Mondrian Los Angeles,
West Hollywood: The
views and crisp-white,
early-2000s vibe have
made this poolside
a mainstay for cocktails
and people watching.
morganshotelgroup.com

03 Mr C Beverly Hills,
Beverly Hills: The
Mr C cocktail – a citrus,
prosecco and vodka pick-
me-up – is a complex
descendant of the Bellini
which was created by
the great-grandfather
of the hotel's founders,
the Cipriani brothers.
Be prepared: known
for its pool parties, the
Mr C hotel is more lively
than relaxing most
summer afternoons.
mrchotels.com

04 Figueroa Hotel,
Downtown: Reopened
in 2016 after a full refresh,
the poolside has been
restored to its original
Spanish theme for
a minimalist and
contemporary
Mediterranean feel.
The historic 1926
property first opened
as a women-only hotel
but is blissfully gender-
inclusive these days.
hotelfigueroa.com

④

The Standard, West Hollywood
Old-school cool

The mid-century modern Standard Hollywood, with its bright blue-and-white colour scheme, opened on the Sunset Strip in 1999. Yes, it's been around the block but the somewhat in-your-face hotel is an old standby with its casual 1960s vibes. The cobalt AstroTurf poolside, wavy balconies and loud décor still get the job done.

Besides sweeping views of the city from every room, there's regular live music and some wholesome Californian fare to be had from the egg-shaped wicker chairs in the Cactus Lounge (named after its desert mural), as well as a boogie or two happening at on-site nightlife spot Mmhmm.
8300 Sunset Boulevard, 90069
+1 323 650 9090
standardhotels.com

MONOCLE COMMENT: In a city where it can be a challenge to find late-night eats, The Standard's diner-like restaurant Alma is open 24 hours.

5

Petit Ermitage, West Hollywood
Bohemian wonderland

Stefan Ashkenazy's ivy-covered
hotel exudes old European charm.
Its 80 eclectic suites are equipped
with kitchenettes and separate
sitting areas, each designed to
mimic a bohemian pied-à-terre.

The rooftop, which opened
as a private members' club in
2009, is where most of the action
happens: there's a saltwater pool
(that's scented with essence of
damask roses for special
occasions), a dining area and,
adding to the surreal quality of the
hotel, a hummingbird and butterfly
sanctuary. The sunken "Firedeck"
also hosts regular yoga classes and
outdoor film screenings.
8822 Cynthia Street, 90069
+1 310 854 1114
petitermitage.com

MONOCLE COMMENT: Ashkenazy's
personal art collection is found
throughout the hotel and includes
the likes of Erté, Dalí and Miró.

Green space
—
There's a kumquat grove on the roof

6

Palihouse, West Hollywood
Rooms with personality

The West Hollywood branch of the
Palihouse opened in 2008, offering
37 suites and long-stay apartments
equipped with kitchens, dining
rooms and myriad amenities. But it's
the attention to design that sets it
apart. The homely aesthetic is a
blend of mid-century modern and
rustic; the eclectic mix of vintage
furniture and artwork gives each
apartment – from the loft studio to
the suite – a character of its own.

   Guests who prefer to leave their
kitchens can enjoy wholesome
Californian fare in the courtyard
at brasserie Mardi by chef Kris
Tominaga, before winding down
with a cocktail at the rooftop lounge.
8465 Holloway Drive, 90069
+1 323 656 4100
palihousewesthollywood.com

MONOCLE COMMENT: Owner Avi
Brosh gets involved in the interior
design of his properties – he selects
all of the quirky vintage pieces,
artwork and busy fabrics.

Which way to Chateau Marmont? My Starmap says Lassie once stayed there...

⑦ Hotel Covell, Los Feliz
Chapter house

You won't find another hotel near here and you certainly won't find another like it in LA. Set in residential Los Feliz, the intimate five-room guesthouse is set above Bar Covell with the entrance in the rear. Each of the well-appointed rooms was designed to tell a chapter in the life of fictional character, writer-poet George Covell. Chapter 3 covers a stint in 1960s Paris with his long-time French girlfriend; Chapter 5: his daughter Isabel's apartment in 1970/1980s New York. The comfortable suites are equipped with features such as Smeg refrigerators, so long-term stays are encouraged, along with those one-night stopovers in George's life.
4626 Hollywood Boulevard, 90027
+1 323 660 4300
hotelcovell.com

MONCLE COMMENT: Covell's wine bar downstairs boasts 150 wines by the glass (*see page 47*) – and it won't even be a challenge to stumble home.

⑧
The Ace, Downtown
LA landmark

This hotel solidified the Downtown renaissance when it opened in 2014. The Ace is set in the historic United Artists tower (built by Charlie Chaplin, Mary Pickford, Douglas Fairbanks and DW Griffith), a 1927 building that's a jewel in the still-gritty city centre. Grec Architects and design firm Commune oversaw the transformation, keeping some of its aged elements while restoring other pieces of the ornate, gothic structure.

The 182 guest rooms stick to what the Ace has become renowned for: rooms are equipped with vinyl, Martin guitars, Pendleton blankets and Pearl+ soaps. Talent from New York was brought in for the LA Chapter restaurant, the rooftop can be a scene and the jaw-dropping theatre is not to be missed (even if it's just to take in the incredible architecture; *see page 115*).
929 South Broadway, 90015
+1 213 623 3233
acehotel.com

MONOCLE COMMENT: Look out for the pencil drawings by the Haas Brothers on the walls of the hotel, featuring an eclectic array of LA characters from Snoop Dogg to Britney Spears.

Bright lights

The Ace's neon 'Jesus Saves' sign is a remnant left over from a time when the property served as part of the Church of the Open Door, presided over by the televangelist Dr Gene Scott, who broadcast his Sunday services from the building.

Jam-packed
—
Check out the Ace's busy calendar of events

Halls of fame
It inspired the Eagles song 'Hotel California'

⑨
Chateau Marmont,
West Hollywood
Famous and infamous

This LA landmark is sexy, dark and a little mysterious. Every room is a surprise, with vaulted ceilings, elaborate heavy fabrics, the odd crooked lampshade and pillows in need of a fluff. Designed after the Château d'Amboise in the Loire Valley, it was built in 1929 as a deluxe apartment building. Many of the hotel's 63 rooms have maintained their original structure – meaning they include full kitchens and living rooms. The charming cottages and bungalows, set discreetly among the lush plant life on the grounds, offer added privacy.
8221 Sunset Boulevard, 90046
+1 323 656 1010
chateaumarmont.com

MONOCLE COMMENT: Plenty of mischievous nights have been had at Chateau Marmont – including Led Zeppelin riding their motorcycles through the halls.

Those rockstars party hard: I'm dog tired

⑩
The Charlie, West Hollywood
Chaplin's retreat

Set in a residential section of West Hollywood, nearly hidden from view, The Charlie is a surprising find with its 14 English-style bungalows immersed in overgrown gardens. Originally built in 1924 and formerly owned by Charlie Chaplin, the property has had a storied past but fell into disrepair until Menachem Treivush discovered it while roaming down Sweetzer Avenue in 2002. It's been brought back to life and the original architecture salvaged, including the stained-glass windows. The grounds have lovely areas in which to dine outside and some of the cottages have private terraces.
819 North Sweetzer Avenue, 90069
+1 323 988 9000
thecharliehotel.com

MONOCLE COMMENT: Chaplin commissioned a slew of European-inspired buildings in LA – check out the French Formosa Cottages and the Normandie Towers.

Three more hotels

01 Shutters on the Beach, Santa Monica: As its name suggests, this elegant Santa Monica institution makes the most of its beach-front location. Many of its rooms look out onto the Pacific, a view shared by its two restaurants and spacious lounge bar.
shuttersonthebeach.com

02 Mondrian Los Angeles, West Hollywood: Given a makeover in 2008 by designer Benjamin Noriega-Oritz, this hotel exudes a sleek and playful sense of style, with rooms that offer a nice line in understated luxury. Make time for a cocktail at the rooftop poolside Skybar and drink in one of the best views in LA.
morganshotelgroup.com

03 The London, West Hollywood: Sprinkled with homages to its British namesake – from an offer of free calls to London landlines to the Vivienne Westwood-designed penthouse suite – this hotel is still the epitome of Californian cool: laidback, luxurious and quietly glamorous.
thelondonwesthollywood. com

Ⓤ
Palihouse, Santa Monica
Moor to enjoy

Palihouse founder Avi Brosh transformed the 1927 Embassy Apartments into his mini-chain's Santa Monica outpost in 2013.

The building is a unique specimen of Moorish-influenced Mediterranean revival architecture. It features a mix of 38 spacious suites and longer-term residences, featuring all the amenities of its Hollywood sibling (*see page 22*).

During the extensive redesign, the team preserved the art nouveau fireplaces, tiled courtyards and oak-beamed ceilings. Additional touches such as vintage-print wallpaper from LA-based Abnormals Anonymous help echo the charm of the era.
1001 3rd Street, 90403
+1 310 394 1279
palihousesantamonica.com

MONOCLE COMMENT: Tucked away a few blocks back from the beach, the Palihouse is pleasantly devoid of any of the cheesy flash that you'll find on the boardwalk.

⑫
The Beverly Hills Hotel, Beverly Hills
In the pink

The Beverly Hills Hotel's pink-and-green motif, 1940s style and banana-leaf wallpaper are iconic and we'd be remiss not to mention them. The 208-room hotel is set on five hectares in LA's most famous area code: 90210. The 23 uniquely designed bungalows are particularly noteworthy; many of their suites are outfitted with silk bathrobes and pianos, and some boast private pools.

The hotel has its share of stories (most recently, a celebrity boycott over its owner the Sultan of Brunei's support for homophobic legislation). Its restaurant, The Polo Lounge, has also been a popular spot for generations – order the famous McCarthy salad.
9641 Sunset Boulevard, 90210
+1 310 276 2251
dorchestercollection.com

MONOCLE COMMENT: Try to snag booth 1 at the Polo Lounge – it was Charlie Chaplin's favourite.

Food and drink
— Savouring the city

LA's food scene is thriving. The weather helps: a Mediterranean climate and close proximity to the fertile Central Valley means that the freshest ingredients wind up on your plate. Then, of course, there are those heaven-sent grapevines.

The city has also become a magnet for nationwide talent in recent years. And while Mexico has exerted the punchiest and most palpable influence on the flavours favoured by Angelenos, the contributions of the Korean, Japanese and Chinese communities have been hefty too. It all adds up to a heady mix.

There's something for everyone, from hip haunts on the city's east side to laidback venues on the shores of Venice and Santa Monica in the west, with plenty of Hollywood glitz and old-school glamour in between.

While at times you may be caught off-guard by an early closing, you'll never suffer a shortage of places to wine and dine in Los Angeles.

Restaurants
Top tables

①
Alimento, Silver Lake
Intimate Italian

LA native Zach Pollack was studying architecture in Florence when he decided to switch his focus to food. He opened Alimento in 2014, a low-key but polished restaurant in Silver Lake that serves regional Italian dishes, from the obscure to the familiar, alongside a strong list of tasty natural wines. Grab a table on the ivy-clad patio and sample some of Pollack's signature pasta, freshly made each day – the tortellini in *brodo* (broth), hailing from Bologna, would be the highlight of any menu.
1710 Silver Lake Boulevard, 90026
+1 323 928 2888
alimentola.com

Food that sings
—
The Thai dishes hit notes of spice

2

Night + Market Song, Silver Lake
Hot stuff

Young chef Kris Yenbamroong (*pictured right*) cut his culinary teeth at his family's restaurant. What you'll find at his own place is authentic, spicy Thai food and a convivial atmosphere. *Aharn glam lao* is the name of the game here, which roughly translates as "food that facilitates drinking and having fun among friends". The decor is kooky, the Singha beer classic and the neighbourhood vibes real. You can't go wrong with the larb (a classic minced-meat salad) but be prepared for the heat packed into all of Yenbamroong's dishes.
3322 West Sunset Boulevard, 90026
+1 323 665 5899
nightmarketsong.com

(3)

Sushi Gen, Little Tokyo
Catch this fish

This hole-in-the-wall sushi
restaurant, set in a less-than-
picturesque strip mall, is a rare gem;
authentic, unpretentious and serving
some of the best sushi in town. Step
inside and try to claim a coveted
table or a spot at the lengthy wooden
sushi bar. Then watch (and eat) as
the meticulous, white-clad chefs roll
out salmon-skin makis, fatty-tuna
sushi, sea bream sprinkled with
lemon and salt, and scallop sashimi
served in the shell. A nice touch
are the complimentary terry cotton
towelettes that you would receive in
Tokyo to cleanse your hands.
422 East 2nd Street, 90012
+1 213 617 0552
sushigen-dtla.com

Must-try
Banana split from Van
Leeuwen, various venues
This ice-cream company may
be an import from Brooklyn but
it's now firmly settled in Los
Angeles, with shops in the Arts
District, Culver City and Franklin
Village, plus multiple trucks on
the road. The banana split is
exactly what Van Leeuwen is all
about: keeping it classic with
simple, high-quality ingredients.
vanleeuwenicecream.com

La familia grande
—
Broken Spanish has a
little sister, BS Taquería,
located a few blocks away. It's
more casual and open all day
but it offers the same house-
pressed heirloom-corn tortillas
and homely atmosphere.
bstaqueria.com

(4)
Broken Spanish, Downtown
Mexican with a twist

It takes guts to open a restaurant
in a quiet part of Downtown (near
Staples Center) – and evenings
only to boot – but that's exactly
what chef Ray Garcia has done,
serving hearty Mexican cuisine
with a refined twist. "This is a
personal story of a third-generation
Angeleno of Mexican descent,"
says Garcia. "We like to say that
we're authentically inauthentic."
The tortillas, made in-house,
are mind-blowing. Also try the
chochoyotes (dumplings with fried-
potato garnish in a garlicky, spicy
broth) or the tender rabbit main.
1050 South Flower Street, 90015
+1 213 749 1460
brokenspanish.com

 ⑤
Cassia, Santa Monica
Popular pan-Asian

Le Cordon Bleu-trained chef Bryant Ng teamed up with his wife Kim and restaurateur couple Zoe Nathan and Joshua Loeb for this project. A celebration of Southeast Asian cuisine – and California's exceptional produce – Cassia is housed in a beautiful 1930s art deco building, the dining room of which can hold up to 200. We'd recommend the *kaya* (coconut jam) toast or any of the dishes made with seafood caught fresh on the Cali coast. The spicy laksa soup and Vietnamese *pot au feu* (beef stew) are also top-notch.
1314 7th Street, 90401
+1 310 393 6699
cassiala.com

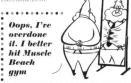
Oops, I've overdone it. I better hit Muscle Beach gym

⑦
Petit Trois, Hollywood
A little piece of Paris

Ludo Lefebvre's homage to the bistros he left behind in his native France may seem incongruously placed given its strip-mall location. Once you cross the threshold of this intimate 22-seater, however, it's as if you've been transported to Paris.

At marble-topped counters, French classics such as steak tartare and escargots are served alongside a carefully chosen selection of wines. The inspired cocktail list is the only giveaway that outside the door is Hollywood and not the Left Bank.
718 Highland Avenue, 90038
+1 323 468 8916
petittrois.com

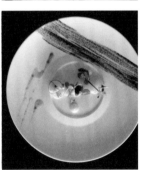

⑥
N/naka, Palms
Lucky 13

Niki Nakayama (*pictured, on left*) is arguably Japan's most celebrated female chef. Her restaurant N/naka specialises in *kaiseki* – a traditional multi-course meal – and features dishes such as *uni*-butter sea bass along with classic sashimi. Despite *kaiseki*'s historic heritage, Nakayama's version is fresh and modern. The dishes centre on seasonal ingredients (with greenery from the chef's own garden) so the menu changes regularly, as do the many wines and sakés that complement it.
3455 South Overland Avenue, 90034
+1 310 836 6252
n-naka.com

8 Ostrich Farm, Echo Park
Elegant comfort food

This restaurant, opened in late 2014 by husband-and-wife team Jaime Turrey and Brooke Fruchtman, is a place to linger – as demonstrated by the constant teeming of devout patrons. The simple elegance of the space – whitewashed walls, inviting green banquettes and brass fixtures – combined with comforting dishes such as creamy polenta and roast chicken keep it welcoming despite the potential wait time. It's Fruchtman's keen eye that's responsible for the interiors while we have Turrey's palate to thank for the menu.
1525 West Sunset Boulevard, 90026
+1 213 537 0657
ostrichfarmla.com

Am I being fattened up? Are you sure this isn't an owl farm?

Bakeries

In Los Angeles the humble loaf has experienced a renaissance over the past few years. Here's our pick of places for naturally leavened breads, buttery morning pastries and fruit-stuffed specialties.

01 Superba Food + Bread, Venice: This Venice outlet has a wide range of baked goods on offer in its oversized industrial space (that doubles as a casual-fare restaurant). Superba serves everything from classic sourdough to *pain au levain* and while pretzel croissants sound like sins against classic pastry, they work.
superbafoodandbread.com

02 Larder Baking Company, various locations: As a child at a boarding school in Venezuela, master baker Nathan Dakdouk would spy on nuns baking bread in the night. Today he's baking a lengthy list of some of LA's best loaves, including rye and caraway, and a blueberry boule packed with fruit.
larderbakingco.com

03 Lodge Bread, Culver City: Organic, wholegrain, long-fermented, high-hydration loaves are what you'll find at the bakery run by Or Amsalam, Alexander Phaneuf and Alan Craig. This dedicated bunch is all about producing very dark, Euro-inspired bread from a Bassanina oven. The Sunday-night pizzas made from superior dough are a highlight.
lodgebread.com

9 Bar Amá, Downtown
Tempting Tex-Mex

Chef Josef Centeno opened this bar-cum-restaurant, his second venture in Downtown, in 2012. It's a tribute to his mother and grandmother for their culinary inspirations (*amá* means "mother"), with a menu rooted in casual Tex-Mex cuisine. The cashew *queso* (cheese) is popular, as are the hefty enchiladas. If you're after lighter fare the snapper with chimichurri will do the trick. Then there are the signature tequila-based drinks; we recommend The Nacho (tequila blanco with a chilli-lime shrub, Campari, citrus and honey).
118 West 4th Street, 90013
+1 213 687 8002
bar-ama.com

Meaty treats

Bestia's charcuterie is made on-site

⑩
Bestia, Arts District
Pizza and pasta perfection

This place is so popular that a reservation may take weeks (so plan ahead). Walk-ins can find space among the ample bar seating: a bonus is the appetite-stimulating view of the woodfired oven baking the pizzas – doughy slices of heaven. Husband-and-wife owners Ori Menashe and Genevieve Gergis have created a rustic Italian menu with pastas and charcuterie made in-house. The *casarecce al pomodoro* (semolina pasta with tomato, fresh ricotta and basil) and the saffron pasta parcel with braised lamb and pine nuts are true crowd-pleasers.
2121 East 7th Place, 90021
+1 213 514 5724
bestiala.com

⑪
The Larchmont, Larchmont Village
Local favourite

This neighbourhood haunt in a cosy Arts & Crafts house has been serving wholesome fare since 2013. Chef Michael Bryant's cuisine is California-meets-Europe: a small, seasonal menu inspired by his southern upbringing and French roots. While the kitchen is known for its harissa scallops and charred octopus, Bryant's traditional fried chicken is also a perennial favourite.

The restaurant has quite a following among celebrities so tables can be scarce. Not to worry: barman Chris Kramer will mix you a cocktail as you wait on the patio.
5750 Melrose Avenue, 90038
+1 323 464 4277
thelarchmont.com

Tacos

01 Guisados, Boyle Heights: Tacos don't come much more authentic than this. The signage is underwhelming but the food will impress, especially the stewed-meat tacos.
guisados.co

02 Villa Moreliana, Downtown: The menu may be small but that doesn't stop the punters from queuing up to sample what are perhaps LA's finest *carnitas* (slow-cooked pork inspired by the traditions of Michoacan).
grandcentralmarket.com

03 Ricky's Fish Tacos, East Hollywood: This food truck is something of a legend. Serving the East Hollywood, Los Feliz and Silver Lake catchment area, it's where to go if you've had enough of meat-heavy tacos; fillings include fish, prawn and even lobster.
The truck is usually at 1400 North Virgil Avenue

12

Baroo, Hollywood
Good Korea move

At first glance this South Korean venue doesn't seem that promising a prospect: it's cheap as chips, tiny and located in a mall. Happily though, Baroo exceeds all expectations. The kimchi fried rice – with its *sous vide* poached egg, gremolata and pineapple-jalapeño salsa – or the spicy oxtail ragú with homemade noodles could easily grace the tables of any fine-dining establishment. Kwang Uh (*pictured, left*) and partner Matthew Kim don't skimp on visuals, ingredients or flavour.
5706 Santa Monica Boulevard, 90038
+1 323 819 4344
baroola.strikingly.com

13

Wolf, West Hollywood
Edible artistry

Chef Marcel Vigneron opened Wolf in early 2016. The decor and the music may be a little flashy for our tastes but the dishes come out of the kitchen bursting with flavour.

"We want our food and culture to capture the zeitgeist that makes up modern-day Los Angeles," says Vigneron. The beetroot is dressed like a work of art, the cod sits beautifully in a flavourful broth and the burnt carrots are cooked to perfection. And then there are the crispy potatoes... Light as air on the inside with a perfectly crunchy exterior.
7661 Melrose Avenue, 90046
+1 323 424 7735
wolfdiningla.com

14
Norah, West Hollywood
Outstanding food and service

Norah opened amid much fanfare in early 2016. Despite its expansive space on Santa Monica Boulevard it doesn't miss on making guests feel welcome. The menu is also surprising: adventurous yet accessible. The food changes slightly every day but look out for the *uni*-butter poached prawn and cauliflower popcorn; or consider going all-in with the tasting menu.

There is some questionable art on the walls but that's a minor detail compared to the outstanding food and service.
8279 Santa Monica Boulevard, 90046
+1 323 450 4211
norahrestaurant.com

Walk-in style
—
Norah is perpetually popular, not least because of its knowledgable and friendly staff. When the restaurant is fully booked with reservations grab a seat at the bar; it's also possible to stroll in and score a place at the high-top communal tables.

Juice bars

In a city as obsessed with health and beauty as LA, it's no surprise that Angelenos go wild for cold-pressed juices. Here's our pick of the best spots for a fresh squeeze.

01 Juice Served Here, citywide: Given the fashion-industry backgrounds of founders Alex Matthews and Greg Alterman, it's not surprising that the packaging of LA's most beloved juice chain is so pleasing to the eye. The juices live up to the hype and friendly staff are always happy to assist, whether you're after a cleansing green number or a creamy Super Choc smoothie made with nuts and cacao.
juiceservedhere.com

02 Moon Juice, citywide: This chain borders on parody, with its all-white interiors and fresh-faced staff. With product names such as Blue Moon Protein and Sex Dust, Moon Juice truly has the most "exotic" selection of juices around.
moonjuiceshop.com

03 Café Gratitude, citywide: This brand may have some hippie tendencies but the juices are delicious and the staff charming. If you're on the picky side, they may even be kind enough to make you a special concoction of your own. Don't be alarmed if it comes with an affirmation from your server.
cafegratitude.com

Gjelina, Venice
Brunch bonanza

This is something of a Venice institution and a brand in its own right; Gjusta bakery (*see page 43*) is from the same team. The decor is modern, if a little generic, but what brings the punters here in their hordes is the cuisine. Good for brunch, the menu is extensive – think everything from porridge to pizzas – meaning you're sure to find something toothsome. The Moroccan baked eggs with merguez sausage, swimming in tomato sauce with yoghurt and coriander, will bust any hangover.
1429 Abbot Kinney Boulevard, 90291
+1 310 450 1429
gjelina.com

Pot, Koreatown
Choi's morsels

This venue is a tribute to South Korean cuisine and culture courtesy of Roy Choi, whose CV includes pioneering the food-truck revolution in LA and inventing the Korean taco. Pot opened in 2014 in the polychrome Line Hotel and has delectable dishes from kimchi to hickory-smoked duck breast. The noodle-based hot pots are the main event and though the ingredients may seem haphazard there's method to Choi's madness. The restaurant also holds events such as Tribe Taco Tuesday, a mellow evening of live music, tacos and cocktails.
3515 Wilshire Boulevard, 90010
+1 213 368 3030
eatatpot.com

Gracias Madre, West Hollywood
Natural appeal

Gracias Madre's elegant interior – with its tiled bar and natural lighting – may distract you from the fact that you're looking at a plant-based menu. But it's not a smokescreen: the food makes this a firm favourite among omnivores and herbivores alike. Think hearty vegetable tacos and potato-masa cakes with salsa.

Beverage director Jason Eisner brings a dizzying number of small-batch mezcals and tequilas to the spirits list, plus an inventive range of cocktails (including a non-psychoactive line made with cannabis essential oils).
8905 Melrose Avenue, 90069
+1 323 978 2170
graciasmadreweho.com

Nothing like a tequila cocktail to stimulate an appetite for tacos

Matsuhisa, Beverly Hills
Nobu prototype

Before Nobu made chef Nobuyuki
Matsuhisa an internationally fêted
name, he was using his surname
(as opposed to his nickname) for
this establishment. The chef started
his eponymous US restaurant in
the late 1980s after stints in South
America and Alaska, and it's
still a classic today. The exterior
is unassuming but the food is
phenomenal. The long menu
of hot and cold dishes can be
overwhelming so we recommend
the *omakase* menu – a selection of
Matsuhisa's best signature creations.
*129 North La Cienega
Boulevard, 90211
+1 310 659 9639
nobumatsuhisa.com*

République, La Brea
Polished classics

Both Margarita and Walter
Manzke have first-rate culinary
backgrounds from time spent
in top kitchens around the
world. République serves classic
(perhaps a little safe) fodder
but what it does, it does well.
There are dishes such as perfectly
al dente pappardelle with pork
ragout and rack of lamb from
Northern Cali's Marin Sun Farms.
   The temple-like building,
constructed in 1928 by Charlie
Chaplin and designed by architect
Roy Sheldon Price has a grand
tiled courtyard and gabled ceiling.
*624 South La Brea Avenue, 90036
+1 310 362 6115
republiquela.com*

Bread & breakfast

In a city where diners can be a
little squeamish about gluten,
the breads, brioches and
croissants on République's
breakfast menu are a rare
indulgence. It's all thanks
to the restaurant's French
influence – and to the artistry
of owner Margarita.

Coffee
Perfect perks

Blacktop, Arts District
Top-notch brews

Blacktop's coffee, expertly crafted
by some of the city's best baristas,
will draw you to this neighbourhood
spot like a magnet. By the time
owner Tyler Wells opened the shop
in 2014 he had already made a
name for himself in the business;
his previous project, Handsome
Coffee Roasters, had been famed
for its anti-sugar policy. "Blacktop
is simpler," says Wells. "It's just
a little pavement café." And this
straightforward approach is what
makes the place ideal for a cup of
cold brew after a morning perusing
the local art spaces.
*826 East 3rd Street, 90013
+1 213 599 8496
blacktop.la*

Keen beans
Verve also has an outpost in Japan

Of course I drink coffee, I'm nocturnal

②

Verve Coffee Roasters, Downtown
Caffeine and juice

Verve coffee can be found across LA, although its headquarters and roasters are in Santa Cruz. Owners Ryan O'Donovan and Colby Barr learned the ropes at a series of other ventures before starting their own business in 2007. The duo is committed to sourcing quality beans from around the world, with a focus on Latin America and Africa. Their industrial-looking shop in Downtown was designed by Studio MAI and does double duty as a coffee house and juicery in conjunction with Juice Served Here (*see page 36*).
833 South Spring Street, 90014
+1 213 455 5991
vervecoffee.com

③ Bondi Harvest, Santa Monica
Wizards of Oz

This Sydney import came to Los Angeles in spring 2016 and the laidback café turns out perfect Aussie flat whites and healthy brekkies. Owners Mark Alston and Guy Turland keep the menu simple and clean, serving dishes such as quinoa and coconut-cream porridge or the Rad Bowl with chimichurri-dressed cauliflower rice and fermented vegetables. Though it's not that close to the shore, the whitewashed interior packs the vibe of a seaside shack – and the atmosphere is enough to make you feel like you're hanging out down under.
1814 Berkeley Street, 90404
+1 310 586 7419
bondiharvest.cafe

④ Go Get Em Tiger, Larchmont Village
Roar appeal

Kyle Glanville and Charles Babinski deliver the highest-quality cups without the pretention that can often accompany serious brewing. They trawl samples from hundreds of roasters, selecting favourites through blind tasting, and the result is a diverse menu of the best roasts available. Their first location – at Grand Central Market, under the name G&B – has a bar-service feel but this Larchmont space provides a small breakfast and lunch menu and room for you to linger.
230 North Larchmont Boulevard, 90004
+1 323 380 5359
gandb.coffee

⑤ Flowerboy Project, Venice
Mixed bunch

Flowerboy Project – opened by long-time Venice resident Sean Knibbs in summer 2015 – packs a lot in. Part flower shop, part boutique, part coffeehouse, it sells an eclectic mix of goods, including pale-hued ceramics, notebooks from Public Supply, perfumes from Fiele Fragrances and house-made nut butters. The Vittoria coffee is served alongside pastries from various suppliers and a selection of toasts (the tahini offering, topped with sesame, ground hibiscus and thyme, is as good as it sounds).
824 Lincoln Boulevard, 90291
+1 310 452 3900
flowerboyproject.com

Lunch
Midday pit stops

① Winsome, Echo Park
Sunshine on Sunset

Set in a residential building in Echo Park, Winsome is slightly off the beaten path – but it's well worth going out of your way to find this sunny restaurant. The interior is sleek and pretty; its caramel-hued booths are inviting and the lengthy bar has ample seating to view the magic in the kitchen. There's also a large open patio on which to soak up the rays. As to chef Jeremy Strubel's menu, it's straightforward and simple but all of the dishes are packed with flavour. The excellent burger alone makes Winsome a choice spot.
1115 Sunset Boulevard, 90012
+1 213 415 1818
eatwinsome.com

Old country
Brentwood
Country Mart
opened in the
1940s

②
Farmshop, Santa Monica
California cuisine

Set in the quaint Brentwood
Country Mart, Farmshop is
part restaurant, part speciality
grocers. "I wanted to create
a restaurant focused on local
producers and artisans," says
chef and owner Jeff Cerciello,
formerly of Thomas Keller's
restaurant group. Under culinary
director Brian Reimer (*pictured,
below*), Farmshop serves California-
inspired food: think crispy
artichokes with burrata and
pesto, and marinated Pacific
sardines. It's best in the day
while the market is buzzing.
*225 26th Street, Suite 25, 90402
+1 310 566 2400
farmshopca.com*

*Picnic? I prefer to say
I'm dining owl fresco*

041

I'm just putting the final touches to my screenplay then it's off to my power lunch

Power lunch

Mixing business with food is perfectly permissible in LA, but rarely outside of office hours: the healthy option of a brisk lunch is preferred over boozy dinners with clients (perhaps because so many Angelenos are anxious to get on the busy freeway to head home). With this in mind, here's our top-three spots for a business lunch.

01 Otium, Downtown: An airy, laidback restaurant with an emphasis on rustic cooking with sustainable ingredients. *otiumla.com*

02 Redbird, Downtown: Located inside a former cathedral rectory, this spacious restaurant is a temple to modern American cuisine. With private-dining options for those business-sensitive meetings. *redbird.la*

03 The Polo Lounge, Beverly Hills: A favoured haunt of celebrities since the 1930s, this Beverly Hills Hotel fixture is the epitome of old-world glamour. *dorchestercollection.com*

Last orders
—
Make sure you order by the 14.00 cut-off

③
Trois Familia, Silver Lake
French-Mexican fusion

French chef Ludo Lefebvre has made quite the buzz around LA with Petit Trois (*see page 32*) and Trois Mec. Next up is Trois Familia, in a nondescript strip mall on Sunset Boulevard (understated locations and frontage are something of a Lefebvre signature). Open for breakfast and lunch only, it's a Mexican-French fusion – although the menu skews towards Mexican. Take some of the more decadent creations, for instance: double-decker potato tacos served with lime, crème fraîche and jack cheese. So wrong, so good.
3510 Sunset Boulevard, 90026
+1 323 725 7800
troisfamilia.com

(5)
Gjusta, Venice
Well bread

Part of the Gjelina empire and the
place where the restaurant's bread
is expertly baked, Gjusta is the
café arm of the hugely successful
main locale on Venice's Abbot
Kinney (*see page 37*). Here it's all
about swift, ticketed service that
is intended to get you up close
and personal with cakes, scones,
cookies and some particularly good
sourdough bread (all teasing you
from behind the glass) as soon as
possible. It's also a decent spot for
breakfast and sandwiches. Perch on
a bar stool inside, or there's outdoor
seating (if you can grab a spot).
320 Sunset Avenue, 90291
+1 310 314 0320
gjusta.com

(4)
Sqirl, Silver Lake
Jam packed

This postage stamp-sized café is
charming, filled with attractive
people and serves easy-going fare.
It's perpetually popular too, which
may mean a bit of a wait – but it's
a small price to pay for the rhubarb
lemonade and the sorrel-pesto
rice bowl. In fact the biggest mark
against Sqirl is that it's only open
until 16.00. The good news is that
breakfast is served all day long to
cater to the varied schedules of
Angelenos. Sqirl's signature jams
can also be found all over the city
(when it first opened in 2011, it was
just a preserves company).
4/720 Virgil Avenue, 90029
+1 323 284 8147
sqirlla.com

Be prepared
———
Whether in the market for
a baklava croissant or lox on
crispy rye toast from Gjusta,
it's a good idea to know your
order before you make it
to the till. This place
is constantly packed and
there's no time for fuss.

043

Grand Central Market
Stall stories

Market stalls

Grand Central Market opened on Broadway in Downtown in 1917 but it's undergone a facelift of sorts over the past few years. Today it's home to a fascinating mix of old and new sellers; here is our pick of the stalls to visit.
grandcentralmarket.com

01 Madcapra: An all-things-vegetable falafel shop? They might limit themselves to plant-based ingredients but Sara Kramer and Sarah Hymanson's dishes jump with flavour and zest. "I feel like the market is the seat of a lot of change in LA so it's exciting to watch that from the inside," says Hymanson. Try the green falafel sandwich, which she describes as "not traditional at all".
Stall B-10

02 La Tostadería: This stall serves delicious seafood, including fish tacos and spicy ceviche. "This is a real Mexican place serving modern cuisine," says founder Fernando Villagomez, who also owns another stand, Villa Moreliana, that focuses on traditional pork carnitas.
Stall E-10

03 China Café: This is one of the oldest stands in the market: it dates from 1959. Try Chinese classics such as chow mein and chop suey. "People tell me they've been coming here since they were babies – and now they're bringing their own families," says owner Rinco Cheung.
Stall C-14

①

The Tower Bar, West Hollywood
Classy classic

Situated in the art deco landmark
Sunset Tower Hotel (*see page 16*), this
bar's walnut-panelled walls, fireplace
and live jazz make a visit feel like a
step back in time. Veteran maître d'
Dimitri Dimitrov keeps the classic
cocktail lounge running smoothly
and is a major reason why it has
become an LA legend; the white-
jacket-clad staff servicing the 80-seat
room are of the highest quality too.

Classic mixes bode well here but
The Dimitri (muddled Luxardo
cherry, gin, spirit Veev and lime) is a
contemporary alternative. Pair it with
an old-school prawn cocktail.
8358 Sunset Boulevard, 90069
+1 323 848 6677
sunsettowerhotel.com

②

Cole's, Downtown
Old school

There's a "hidden" bar out the
back of Cole's that isn't that much
of a secret any more: it feels a little
stilted and, dare we say it, passé.
It's more fun in our book to spend
time in Cole's itself, an old-time bar
founded in 1908 and refurbished in
2008. It's all wooden panelling and
dark-red leather seating but this is no
purveyor of lite beer, friends: it has
some of the best cocktails in town
served by knowledgeable staff. One
such legend was Jimmy Barela, who
tended the bar for 63 years before
retiring in 1983. There's a picture of
him on the wall. Rightfully so.
118 East 6th Street, 90014
+1 213 622 4090
colesfrenchdip.com

Training room
Cole's is the
old HQ of the
Pacific Electric
railway

Covell, Los Feliz
All about the alcohol

This has quickly established itself as a destination bar. Why? Because the co-owners are pretty serious about the drinks, so much so that the food seems merely an afterthought. Covell was opened in 2010 by Dustin Lancaster and Matthew Kaner. The former had worked at Café Stella (*see below*) and the latter had spent time at Silverlake Wine. Covell is the sweet symbiosis of their shared interests, offering eight rotating beers on tap and 150 wines by the glass, all within a rustic-chic, warmly glowing enclave.
4628 Hollywood Boulevard, 90027
+1 323 660 4400
barcovell.com

④
Bar Marmont, West Hollywood
Hollywood legend

The interior of one of LA's best-known cocktail lounges is dripping with old Hollywood glam but manages to stay on the right side of good taste. Tactile fittings – leather couches, tasselled lampshades and plush wall-coverings – and dim lighting create a warm space with a classic feel. Keeping with the theme, the best drinks on the menu are the tried-and-trues, so tuck into a sidecar and sink back into your seat.

Turn up early and you may find yourself with only one or two others at the bar; if you've come here to party, aim to arrive late and in style.
8171 West Sunset Boulevard, 90046
+1 323 650 0575
chateaumarmont.com

⑤
Chez Jay, Santa Monica
Dive inn

There's nothing like a good dive bar, especially if it's in a rather over-polished area such as Santa Monica. Chez Jay is the sort of place where you know the no-nonsense barmaid's name and you can spot the regulars, who stay away from fancy drinks.

It's also in a beer-buzzed time warp; it's been going since 1959 and has seen Hollywood A-listers and the Rat Pack pass through. Movies have been written and rehearsed here but ultimately it's all about having a cold drink at the bar, quietly sheltered from the winds of change outside.
1657 Ocean Avenue, 90401
+1 310 395 1741
chezjays.com

⑥
Café Stella, Silver Lake
Starry nights

Okay, so it may be a little sceney but Café Stella is nonetheless one of the best bars on LA's eastern side. Indeed, with its constantly evolving roster of potent, seasonal cocktails you would be hard-pushed to put a foot wrong with your drinks selection.

The café proper is always buzzing with people tucking into its French-inspired menu but it's in the adjoining bar that the real action takes place. Sip on tipples such as Son of a Priest (made with Willett rare-release rye, Campari and Averna) and take a seat at the bar or on one of the comfy sofas around the flanks. This place tends to get packed most evenings but there's always respite to be found on the pretty outdoor patio if it gets a little overwhelming.
3932 Sunset Boulevard, 90029
+1 323 666 0265
cafestella.com

Retail
— Best in store

As you'd expect from one of the most influential cities in the US, Los Angeles can keep up with the big guns when it comes to fashion. Year-round warm weather and the laidback Californian culture contribute to a distinctive sense of style and the discerning shopper will find plenty of homegrown brands to covet. LA natives and recent converts are dipping into the deep pool of creative talent to offer everything from locally designed denim to ceramics.

The pole of influence may have shifted away from Abbot Kinney in Venice to the city's east side, where neighbourhoods such as Silver Lake and Echo Park are proving their chops, but there are sure-fire retail options all over town, from Culver City to Melrose in West Hollywood. The main trouble you'll have is narrowing down your list of places to visit.

Menswear
LA casual

General Quarters, La Brea
Outdoor chic

If you're the type who likes to look rugged and urban at the same time, General Quarters has you covered. Owner Blair Lucio brings an appreciation for Americana to this small shop that stocks heritage brands such as Red Wing, Filson and Tellason.

Beyond the strong selection of beloved labels, the shop – which first opened in LA in 2010 – is a welcoming place. Quite often you'll find Lucio himself is on hand to greet shoppers.
153 South La Brea Avenue, 90036
+1 323 937 5391
generalquartersstore.com

If the cap fits

Having started out in fashion by trying to design the perfect baseball cap, James Perse has since made a name for himself crafting deceptively casual clothing. The label (which now also includes furniture) sells through its own shops and LA's Bloomingdale's.
jamesperse.com

With my new shades and cruiser bike, I really fit in at Venice

Union, La Brea
Sophisticated streetwear

Union first started slinging out T-shirts in 1989. "It was originally a very 'straight, no chaser' streetwear store," says owner Chris Gibbs, who took the reins in 2008. Today the cult men's shop has evolved to blend everything from Japanese brands such as Visvim and WTAPS to designers such as Raf Simons, Thom Browne and JW Anderson. "As streetwear blew up and became a full-fledged fashion category, Union started to become more and more sophisticated," says Gibbs, "while still keeping its streetwear sensibilities."
110 South La Brea Avenue, 90036
+1 323 549 6950
unionlosangeles.com

Wittmore, Arts District
New on the scene

Formerly of New York, Paul Witt fell so deeply in love with LA while running a pop-up shop some years ago that he opened a permanent Wittmore space and didn't look back. Set in the Arts District, Wittmore carries top-tier casual brands such as Max 'n Chester, Unis, CWST and Officine Générale, alongside a few vintage mid-century furniture pieces, Matsuda eyewear, Weiss watches and quirky Studio Arhoj ceramics. On a lucky day you'll find Witt's canine pal Teddy there.
300 South Santa Fe Avenue,
Suite X, 90013
+1 213 626 0780
shopwittmore.com

④
Apolis: Common Gallery,
Arts District
Clothes and events

Brothers Raan and Shea Parton
were pioneers in the Arts District,
setting up a menswear shop there
in 2007. Their own line, started in
2004, has grown to fill the space,
which also hosts photo exhibitions
and a bi-monthly talks series.
   Many of the items sold here are
made through relationships with
manufacturers in places such as
Uganda, Peru and Bangladesh,
and among the woollen coats and
hand-knitted alpaca jumpers there
are leather accessories, travel bags
and a selection of journals.
806 East 3rd Street, 90013
+1 213 613 9626
apolisglobal.com

⑤
Magasin, Culver City
European influence

Created by Josh Peskowitz (the
former men's fashion director at
Bloomingdale's), Magasin is housed
in the new Platform complex
and carries Japanese and Italian
designers mixed with US and
European brands. "They all share
a passion for fabric development,
sophistication – without playing it
safe – in colour and pattern, and a
willingness to experiment with fit,"
says Peskowitz. "All are appropriate
for a man who needs to be in a
boardroom, an art opening, a rowdy
bar and an airport lounge all in the
course of a day."
8810 Washington Boulevard, 90232
+1 213 458 8424
magasinthestore.com

Womenswear
Dressed to impress

①
LCD, Venice
Stylish surfwear

Geraldine Chung (*pictured*) started
LCD as an online surf shop in 2012.
It's evolved to carry heavy hitting
and lesser-known brands with an
air of sophistication. "Over the
years we've gradually shifted our
focus towards discovering and
supporting the most promising
young emerging designers from
around the world," says Chung.
   The bricks-and-mortar
shop, opened in March 2016,
stocks Ryan Roche hats and
knitwear, indie label Nomia,
jewellery by Gabriela Artigas
and Ahlem eyewear.
1919 Lincoln Boulevard, 90291
+1 424 500 2552
shoplcd.co

②
General Store, Venice
Dress like a local

Serena Mitnik-Miller and Mason
St Peter's shop opened in 2009
in Venice Beach. The shelves are
stocked with goods that represent
the California vibe: understated
and effortlessly cool. Black Crane
jumpsuits and Lauren Manoogian
cotton pieces are complemented
by Earth Tu Face bath products
and bright ceramic mini-cactus
sculptures by artist Wills Brewer.
Not to be missed are the vintage
finds which include denim
items, turquoise jewellery and
photographic journals and books
from the 1960s.
1801 Lincoln Boulevard, 90291
+1 310 751 6393
shop-generalstore.com

Shop fit

With its near-faultless weather
and worshipful attitude towards
the body beautiful, LA is fitness
and health-obsessed. Among
its plentiful sports outlets
we recommend Prana in
Manhattan Beach, which offers
a dizzying array of organic
cotton activewear.
prana.com

④
Dream Collective, Silver Lake
More than decoration

While it's billed as a jewellery shop, there's more going on here than that. Opened in 2012, the boutique houses breezy California womenswear lines such as Lykke Wullf, perfumes by Santa Monica's Fiele and even furniture pieces by Shin Okuda from Waka Waka.

Owner Kathryn Bentley has two in-house jewellery lines: Dream Collective and Kathryn Bentley. Her slightly unpolished works use stones such as opals and black diamonds and even lesser-known tourmaline. There is also a house-made line of enamel barrettes.
1404 Micheltorena Street, 90026
+ 1 323 660 2000
dreamcollective.com

③
TenOverSix, West Hollywood
Secret stash

TenOverSix is almost hidden from view near chic Melrose Place. Founder and creative director Kristen Lee Cole keeps it stocked with treasures: "We focus on independent and emerging design and the intersection of design, art and fashion," says Cole.

Covetable women's fashion and accessories are complemented by objects from designers spanning Los Angeles, Brooklyn, Austin, London, Berlin and Paris. "We just buy what intrigues us," says Cole, "what we want to be wearing and what we want to fill our homes with."
8425 Melrose Avenue, 90069
+ 1 323 330 9355
tenover6.com

Mixed fashion
Egalitarian retail

①

Individual Medley, Atwater Village
Sartorial harmony

The main thoroughfare in Atwater
Village is dotted with everything
you need in life: a good bookshop,
a nice bakery and lunch counter,
and – as of 2012 – Individual
Medley, the perfect boutique for
stylish apparel and a few choice
accessories. Owned by Monica
Navarro and Justin Boyes (*both
pictured*), the shop stocks a
small but well-chosen selection of
casualwear for both men and women
as well as vintage finds (a Japanese
tunic, perhaps?). There's also a
handful of excellent ceramics and
other knick-knacks by artists such
as LA-based Kat + Roger
and A Question of Eagles.
3176 Glendale Boulevard, 90039
+1 323 665 5344
individualmedleystore.com

②

Maxfield, West Hollywood
Art of outfitting

With its high-end aesthetics
and gallery-like space, Maxfield
could be added to your list of
cultural institutions to visit in LA.
It's worth stopping by if only for
a self-guided tour but if you want to
head home with some luxury goods
in your suitcase Maxfield
is stacked. There's Dior and
Comme des Garçons, Junya
Watanabe and Isabel Marant, as
well as vintage Cartier and Hermès
items among many more. Opened
in 1969 by Tommy Perse, Maxfield
has been a definitive LA shopping
experience ever since.
8825 Melrose Avenue, 90069
+1 310 274 8800
maxfieldla.com

③

Mohawk General Store, Silver Lake
A shop for all

Mohawk General Store has two
side-by-side shops on Silver Lake's
main drag: one for menswear and
another for women (plus a location
in Pasadena). There's plenty to
covet in the two spaces: beyond
Mohawk's own line there is apparel
from labels such as Dries Van
Noten, Lemaire, Issey Miyake and
Acne Studios alongside Mohawk's
pick of accessories, small homeware
goods and beauty and grooming
products. The eclectic mix by
owners Kevin and Bo Carney is
not to be missed.
4011-4017 West Sunset
Boulevard, 90029
+1 323 669 1602
mohawkgeneralstore.com

④

American Rag Cie, La Brea
Denim and more

American Rag Cie has been called
a one-stop shop and it's hard
to argue with that assessment.
The space is sprawling and packs
in some serious casualwear,
including brands such as DDUGOFF,
Engineered Garments, Opening
Ceremony and many more. There's
even a hefty portion of the shop
devoted solely to denim (which
includes a dedicated member of
staff at the "denim bar").
   To top everything off, the
shop adjoins homeware retailer
Maison Midi, which has the
charming Café Midi in the back.
150 South La Brea Avenue, 90036
+1 323 935 3154
americanrag.com

SoCal vibe

Ron Herman – a men's
and women's shop – has
been a staple for denim on
Melrose Avenue since 1976.
It showcases brands such
as Dries van Noten, Maison
Kitsuné and Zanerobe, as well
as its own line of denim with a
breezy SoCal aesthetic.
ronherman.com

Concept shops
Mixed goods

*I find a
nice flower
pot really
spruces up
a nest*

8463

①
The Apartment by The Line,
West Hollywood
Home comforts

There may be no place better suited
to house the LA iteration of The
Apartment by The Line than serene
Melrose Place. Creative director
Vanessa Traina brings together
goods that span fashion, home,
beauty and art. Every item in the
pristine collection feels like it belongs
– whether it's the maple and birch
bed by Los Angeles designer Doug
McCollough of DMDM, a simple
Acne Studios top tucked neatly in
the wardrobe, or something from the
collection of bath products atop the
marble vanity.
8463 Melrose Place, 2nd Floor, 90069
+ 1 323 746 5056
theline.com

Just One Eye, Hollywood
Masterful mix

A self-proclaimed "future concept store", this luxury boutique melds the worlds of high fashion and art inside an ivy-clad art deco building once owned by Howard Hughes. It's a bit of a shopping spot but visitors are rewarded with a gallery-like presentation of couture brands and quirky art pieces. Founder Paola Russo brings more than 25 years of experience in the retail business and somehow manages to pull off mixing Alexandre Vauthier with Marni, Damien Hirst and an Edwardian piano bench.
7000 Romaine Street, 90038
+1 888 563 6858
justoneeye.com

③ Alchemy Works, Arts District
Refined homeware

The vintage car in the middle of the shop may draw your attention first but don't be distracted from the small handsome goods on the shelves. Alchemy Works, owned by husband-and-wife team Raan and Lindsay Parton, carries homeware, art, jewellery, vintage goods and even apothecary items discovered on the couple's travels around the globe. "The process is never over," says Lindsay. "This is what keeps us inspired and motivated to refresh the shop with new items." The Partons have a keen eye so there's always something to discover.
826 East 3rd Street, 90013
+1 323 487 1497
alchemyworks.us

④ Poketo, Arts District
Creative collective

Bright and funky, Poketo was opened by Ted Vadakan and Angie Myung (*both pictured*) in 2012. Its simple wooden shelves are decked with well-chosen homeware, books, jewellery and apparel, as well as Poketo's pride and joy: its own line of stationery, the majority of which is designed in LA or through collaborations with artists. In fact Poketo has worked with more than 200 international artists on exclusive products for the shop and brands such as Nike and SF Moma. The beloved retailer can also be found inside The Line hotel.
820 East 3rd Street, 90013
+1 213 537 0751
poketo.com

⑤
County Ltd, Silver Lake
Design allrounder

This shop is owned by four friends
– Phillip Proyce, Taylor Caruso,
Kirill Bergart and Joe Lorens –
with backgrounds in fashion and
hospitality. The group has a taste
for simple pleasures and their
own brands (chunky furniture by
Counter Space and classic Lady
White Co T-shirts) are mixed in
with goods from Tokyo, San
Francisco and New York.
  "We blend the two worlds of
homeware and clothing to create
a retail environment that allows
customers to discover design in
multiple platforms," says Proyce.
1837 Hyperion Avenue, 90027
+ 1 323 741 8337
countyltd.com

Home and interior design
Life enhancing

①
Tortoise General Store, Venice
Slow but steady expansion

Tokyo natives Keiko and Taku
Shinomoto moved to LA in
2003 and shortly after opened a
homeware shop. The husband-
and-wife team then added a gallery
space (now called Tortoise),
connected through a small garden,
to showcase ceramics and art by
Japan-based artists.
  The pair pack the general store
with hard-to-find kitchenware,
stationery and grooming tools,
including boar-hair brushes by
Kanaya Brush, chestnut-hued
leather pencil cases and brass
items by Taku himself.
1208 Abbot Kinney Boulevard, 90291
+ 1 310 314 8448
tortoisegeneralstore.com

Hammer and Spear, Arts District
Striking collection

Hammer and Spear sits in a lofty corner space at the end of the main drag in the Arts District. What began in 2013 as a small showroom on the side of a multidisciplinary design studio has grown to fill the now 500 sq m shopfront.

Husband and wife Scott Jarrell and Kristan Cunningham (*both pictured*) are long-time proponents of the Arts District revival. They delve into their backgrounds as designers to inform their selection of great products and artworks available from Downtown and beyond.
255 South Santa Fe Avenue, 90012
+1 213 928 0997
hammerandspear.com

③ MidcenturyLA, North Hollywood
Scandinavian style

The name says it all: owner David Pierce's shop in Burbank is a vast compendium of restored mid-century furniture primarily from Denmark, Sweden and Norway, as well as a selection from the US. While you'll find renowned pieces by the likes of Hans J Wegner, Orla Mølgaard-Nielsen and Arne Jacobsen, the showroom hosts a number of items of unknown origin, adding a lick of mystery and treasure hunting to an afternoon browse through the cavernous warehouse. There's also an impressive range of art, photography and ceramics.
5333 Cahuenga Boulevard, 91601
+1 818 509 3050
midcenturyla.com

④
Lawson-Fenning, West Hollywood
Grand designs

Designers Glenn Lawson and
Grant Fenning (*both pictured,*
Lawson on left) were inspired by
Old Town Pasadena's embrace of
modern and contemporary design.
What started as a workshop for
them has evolved into a two-storey
flagship in Melrose (as well as
another shop in Silver Lake and a
separate workshop), housing their
own designs plus vintage pieces
and new works from the likes of De
Jong & Co and ceramics by Ben
Medansky. Larger pieces (such as
their plush Ojai chair) are worth
the extra effort to get home.
6824 Melrose Avenue, 90038
+ 1 323 934 0048
lawsonfenning.com

⑥ JF Chen, Hollywood
Global homeware

Born in Shanghai and raised in Hong Kong, Joel Chen has been dealing antiques for more than 40 years. His warehouse-sized gallery showcases mid-century modernist and contemporary furniture, plus a discerning mix from around the world, including Portuguese cabinets, lesser-known works by Danish artist Ole Wanscher and Anglo-Indian colonial-style pieces.

Chen's engagement in the creative scene (collaborating with Eames for a nearly 300-piece collection and lending works to exhibitions) has earned him a golden reputation.
1000 North Highland Avenue, 90038
+1 323 463 4603
jfchen.com

On display
JF Chen has a 2,700 sq m space in Hollywood

⑤ The Good Liver, Arts District
Form and function

The Good Liver's stock is equal parts beautiful, collectible and functional. "Our focus is delivering facts, history and culture alongside the interesting stories behind the products," says owner Bert Youn (*pictured, centre*), a storyboard artist who travelled the world before settling in LA to open his shop.

His goods hail from Japan, the UK, Germany, France, Italy, Spain, Sweden, Norway, South Korea and the US and include everything from wooden Swedish dish brushes and steel garden scissors to Hinoki wine coolers.
705 Mateo Street, 90013
+1 213 947 3141
good-liver.com

⑦ Surfing Cowboys, Venice
Coastal effects

Husband-and-wife duo Wayne and Donna Gunther turned their private collection into a shop in 1996 after a stint as fashion photographers. Their space on Venice Boulevard is a trove of vintage furniture, homewares, artwork and other curios celebrating Californian culture.

The pieces are mixed as a living collection rather than a mere showroom and many have made appearances on Hollywood movie sets. Highlights include surfboards from the 1920s, mid-century armchairs by Drexel and long-necked chimeneas from the 1970s.
12553 Venice Boulevard, 90066
+1 310 915 6611
surfingcowboys.com

⑧ Galerie Half, Fairfax
Half a world of stock

Galerie Half was founded by Cameron Smith and designer Cliff Fong in 2009 to house top vintage finds from the 20th century and beyond. Set on Melrose Avenue, its filled with a wide collection of goods that the duo has amassed on their travels, including European and Scandinavian modern design pieces, art and artefacts from Africa as well as exquisite primitive objects or mid-century lighting. The two have a sharp eye and their space is well-merchandised so a stop here to see the changing stock is always a delight.
6911 Melrose Avenue, 90038
+1 323 424 3866
galeriehalf.com

I guess they'll just have to re-do that window display

Specialist retail
Select stock

① Clare V, Silver Lake
Packed with bags

Clare V's chic and playful accessories mix French and Californian sensibilities. Founder Clare Vivier and her family split time between France and Los Angeles each year. Her Silver Lake shop opened in 2012 and in it you'll find her signature bags, wallets and accessories alongside a handful of books and limited-edition collaborations with brands such as Steven Alan and Equipment. No detail is missed with this "made in LA" label – including a chambray lining in many of the bags.
3339 West Sunset Boulevard, 90026
+1 323 665 2476
clarev.com

② Aether, La Brea
Ready for action

The handsome La Brea flagship of this LA-based adventurewear brand is designed to perfection. The stylish garments are showcased in an expansive, mood-lit space. But it's not only about looks: all of Aether's apparel lives up to the same high standards, especially on the technical side – you can even try out pieces by wearing them into the walk-in freezer.

You'll also find slick Salt sunglasses, Ruby motorcycle helmets and Snow Peak gear so no matter what activities you've got planned, you'll be covered.
161 South La Brea Avenue, 90036
+1 323 746 5147
aetherapparel.com

③ Garrett Leight, La Brea
Eyes on the prize

Sure, there's no shortage of sunnies in California but none really capture the spirit of LA quite like Garrett Leight's eponymous brand. Born and bred in Venice (just like its founder), Garrett Leight California Optical eyewear mixes timeless shapes with sunny West Coast vibes – think mirrored lenses and the option for a soft pink frame. The son of frames designer Larry Leight (founder of Oliver Peoples), the young designer has glasses-making in his DNA. His bright, breezy shop on La Brea Avenue is well worth a visit.
165 South La Brea Avenue, 90036
+1 323 931 4018
garrettleight.com

④ Cookbook, Echo Park
Natural delights

This charming neighbourhood shop opened in the summer of 2010. The teeny greengrocer, founded by Marta Teegan and Robert Stelzner, specialises only in the good stuff: seasonal, local and organic produce, responsibly raised meats and delicious cheeses.

The size may keep the offering small but there's a lot of love between this outlet and its farmers – and there's a top selection of snacks and pantry staples to take home: California-grown nuts, house-made pesto, Bariani olive oil and San Francisco's Sightglass coffee.
1549 Echo Park Avenue, 90026
+1 213 250 1900
cookbookla.com

Street life

In a city that abounds with luxury-brand shops Rodeo Drive still feels special. An impeccably groomed and elegantly rarefied stretch of high-end retail outlets in Beverly Hills, it attracts Hollywood's beautiful people – and tourists out in the hope of some celeb-spotting.

Retail design

It should come as no surprise that aesthetics-obsessed Angelenos have produced some impressive shops in which to showcase their brands. Here are some eye-catching examples.

01 **The Row, West Hollywood:** The discreet nature of The Row's first shop on Melrose Place makes finding it feel like a real discovery. A serene enclosed pool greets guests while, to each side, garments are displayed delicately on hangers. Vintage furniture pieces grace the two rooms.
therow.com

02 **Irene Neuwirth, West Hollywood:** This upscale jewellery shop might easily trick you into believing you've just landed a high tea invitation. The Commune-designed space has all the makings of a dream home: the interior is warm, with beautifully arranged bookshelves, a stocked kitchen and even a portrait of Neuwirth's Labradoodle.
ireneneuwirth.com

03 **Stampd, La Brea:** Designed by genre-bending firm Snarkitecture, this clothes shop is set above street level on retail-dense La Brea Avenue. The streetwear company favours a minimalist look: light-grey travertine spansthe space, with pale walls and black-and-white photographs. The backdrop is so on-point that it's almost hard to decide what's more impressive: the products or the space itself.
stampd.com

⑤
EnSoie, Silver Lake
Prints charming

In 1974 Monique Meier took over the reins of Zürich's Brauchbar & Sons silk house, which supplied fabric to European couturiers. She introduced a scarf collection and collaborated with artists such as Peter Fischli and Luciano Castelli to create the designs.

Today she also owns EnSoie, a retail space filled with bright apparel, accessories, jewellery, ceramics and Meier's own scarves (which are still hand-printed in the Swiss mountains). Her daughter Anna Meier is onboard as creative director.
3333 Sunset Boulevard, 90026
+ 1 323 662 0985
ensoie.com

⑦
Cactus Store, Echo Park
Pointed interest

Founded by nephew-and-uncle duo
Carlos and Johnny Morera (*both
pictured*), this tiny shop is packed
with cacti of all shapes and sizes.
Both "die-hard collectors", they
opened the shop in late 2014
and specialise in rare and exotic
varieties. "We wanted to educate
and share our love for these
ancient plants: they are some of the
most resilient in the world," says
Carlos. "They survive the harshest
conditions and look incredible while
they are at it." Stock comes from
sources such as an old collector's
yard and an Italian greenhouse.
*1505.5 Echo Park Avenue, 90026
+1 213 947 3009
hotcactus.la*

*Learning to perch
on a cactus is a
prickly business,
Monochan...*

⑥
Parabellum, Culver City
Sustainable leathergoods

LA natives Jason Jones and Mike
Feldman founded this leather-goods
company in 2008. "The goal was to
create ethical fine pieces that would
last forever and get better with use,"
says Feldman.
   The shop exclusively uses
tough but supple bison leather, an
underutilised by-product of the meat
industry. Feldman and Jones built the
domestic supply chain to source the
hides which are tanned and finished
by hand to create timeless belts,
wallets, handbags and even furniture.
*8840 West Washington
Boulevard, 90232
+1 323 852 0800
parabellum.la*

① Arcana: Books on the Arts,
Culver City
New and rarer reads

Lee Kaplan opened this high-end
art-and-design bookshop in 1984.
The quiet space is almost hidden
from view in Culver City, where
it moved in 2012, and it's well
worth searching out. Inside there's
a healthy collection of both out-
of-print and new titles, with an
emphasis on rare and collectible
modern and contemporary art
and photography, not to mention
sections dedicated to fashion
photography, African and African-
American art, graffiti and even surf
and skate culture.
8675 Washington Boulevard, 90232
+ 1 310 458 1499
arcanabooks.com

⑧
Mollusk Surf Shop, Silver Lake
Good vibrations

The Mollusk brand was founded in
2005 in San Francisco by married
couple John McCambridge and
Johanna St Clair. A love of surfing
is at the heart of their operation
here: Mollusk's boards are shaped
by hand in California, as are the
casual apparel and suits. You'll
also find relaxed gear from US
brands such as Topo Designs and,
of course, the odd *Surfer's Journal*
by the register. Even if you don't
invest in a board, Mollusk's sporty
swimwear can keep you looking fit
on the beach.
3511 West Sunset Boulevard, 90026
+ 1 323 928 2735
mollusksurfshop.com

②
The Last Bookstore, Downtown
Titles of all types

This is a prime place to get lost
in the stacks. Opened in 2009,
the expansive corner space in
the Crocker Bank (the shop
relocated there in 2011) houses
a whopping collection of owner
Josh Spencer's favourite things:
books, vinyl and movies.
    Beyond new editions, there
are collectible books as well as
some vintage records. "We strive
to have something for everyone
– whether it's a first edition for
a collector or the newest releases
for an avid reader," says manager
Katie Orphan.
453 South Spring Street, 90013
+ 1 213 488 0599
lastbookstorela.com

Pen pals
—
There's a club here for lovers of signed first editions

③
Skylight Books, Los Feliz
Paper purveyors

Skylight Books, located on one of Hollywood's main thoroughfares, has been a staple in the area for a couple of decades. As well as selling a grand gamut of books, the store organises about 300 events a year.

Perhaps of most interest is the smaller "Part Deux Arts Annex" shop, a couple of numbers down from the original player. The annex has an excellent range of art and design books, graphic novels, music and film tomes and a newsstand of independent magazines, both local and from further afield.

1814 & 1818 North Vermont
Avenue, 90027
+1 323 660 1175
skylightbooks.com

Neighbourhood hit list

In a city this sprawling you need to be strategic about your plan of attack when shopping. To make things a tad easier, we've grouped our favourite shops by area below:

01 Arts District:
Alchemy Works
Apolis
Hammer and Spear
Poketo
The Good Liver
Wittmore

02 Culver City:
Arcana: Books on the Arts
Magasin
Parabellum

03 Echo Park:
Cactus Store
Cookbook

04 Hollywood:
JF Chen
Just One Eye

05 La Brea:
Aether
American Rag Cie
Garrett Leight
General Quarters
Stampd
Union

06 Silver Lake:
Clare V
County Ltd
Dream Collective
EnSoie
Mohawk General Store
Mollusk Surf Shop

07 Venice:
LCD
Surfing Cowboys
Tortoise General Store

08 West Hollywood:
The Apartment by the Line
Irene Neuwirth
Lawson-Fenning
Maxfield
The Row
TenOverSix

Things we'd buy
—— LA's most covetable items

Los Angeles is a shopper's paradise. There are quirky boutiques aplenty, a budding design scene filled with ceramicists and woodworkers and a sunny surf culture that provides a fresh selection of shades and swimwear every season.

You'll no doubt want to take some of those breezy West Coast vibes home with you so we've scoured the territory (tucking a few things into our own luggage on the way) to find the very best that the city has to offer, from artisanal jam and locally-grown almonds to more refined items from the likes of hip retailer Poketo and shoemaker The Palatines.

Don't forget about the classic cobalt-blue Dodgers cap; not only is it an excellent way to keep the California sun from your eyes, it makes for the perfect keepsake too.

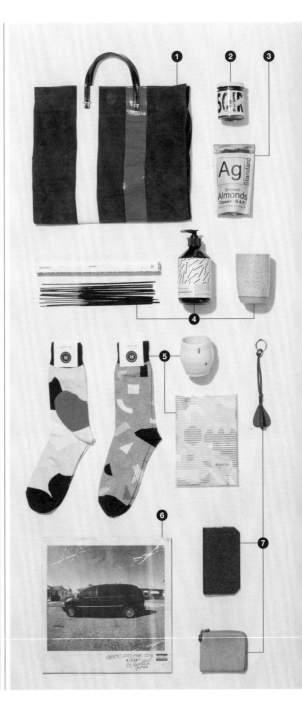

01 Tote from Clare V
clarev.com
02 Rutiz blackberry and
lemon verbena jam by Sqirl
sqirlla.com
03 California almonds
by Ag Standard
getagstandard.com
04 Incense, soap and candle
from Norden Goods
nordengoods.com
05 Socks, ceramic tumbler
and notebook from Poketo
poketo.com
06 Kendrick Lamar vinyl
from Amoeba Music
amoeba.com
07 Leather goods by
Parabellum
parabellum.la
08 Kat & Roger ceramics
from General Store
shop-generalstore.com
09 Sunglasses by Garrett
Leight California Optical
garrettleight.com
10 Skincare essentials by
Earth Tu Face
earthtuface.com
11 Swimwear and beach
blanket by Mollusk
mollusksurfshop.com
12 Venice Cold Brew coffee
venicecoldbrew.com
13 Chocolate by Compartés
compartes.com
14 Sandals by The Palatines
thepalatinesshoes.com

01 Trainers by Vans
vans.com
02 Scarves by Block Shop
blockshoptextiles.com
03 Scents by Fiele Fragrances
fielefragrances.com
04 Aloe vera liqueur by Chareau
chareau.us
05 LA Dodgers hat
losangeles.dodgers.mlb.com

06 *The RKO Story* book from
The Last Bookstore
lastbookstorela.com
07 Wooden cups by De Jong & Co
dejongandco.com
08 Fleetwood Mac vinyl from
Amoeba Music
amoeba.com
09 Men's clothing by James Perse
jamesperse.com

12 essays
—— Lifting the lid on Los Angeles

I'm a writer too, I'm working on my first screenplay: a sequel to 'Birdman'

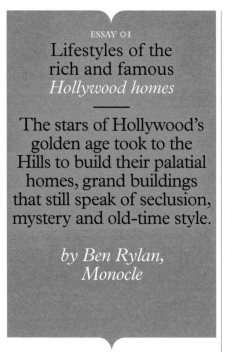

ESSAY 01

Lifestyles of the rich and famous
Hollywood homes

The stars of Hollywood's golden age took to the Hills to build their palatial homes, grand buildings that still speak of seclusion, mystery and old-time style.

by Ben Rylan, Monocle

"It's within these walls that the city's character was crafted – studios started, classics created and dreams destroyed"

I was seated at a street-side table on Sunset Boulevard, seeking refuge from the Californian sun by way of an oversized iced tea. As I sipped the cold nectar, I overheard a nearby tourist wonder aloud where the famous mansion seen in Billy Wilder's 1950 classic film *Sunset Boulevard* might be located. It reminded me of Joe Gillis (played by William Holden) dismissing Norma Desmond's sprawling residence as "a great big white elephant of a place, the kind crazy movie people built in the crazy 1920s".

My first visit to Los Angeles came long after that house had been replaced by an office tower. I'd just caught a screening of the classic film noir *Too Late For Tears* and scenes of its star Lizabeth Scott driving frantically around a dimly lit 1940s Hollywood were still fresh in my mind. I wondered about the view Scott, as one of the few surviving members of old Hollywood, must have had of the city's evolution from her long-time home in the Hills.

The area of Los Angeles known as Hollywood is really a small player in the city's wider urban landscape. But it symbolises far more than a location; its movies gave the city its mythology, and it's the people tucked away behind the closed doors of those mysterious Hollywood Hills homes who give the town its legends. Indeed, it's within those walls that the city's character was crafted – studios started, classics created and dreams destroyed.

Scott stopped making films in the mid-1950s and had rarely given interviews since then though I had heard that she often responded by post to queries that piqued her interest. Although I knew an interview was out of the question, I'd exchanged letters with Scott and she'd agreed to a meeting at her home. Leaving behind the grid of downtown Hollywood I tucked away my map and headed for the Hills. Like Rome's Colosseum rising above the chaotic and evolving city around it, many of the old structures of Valley Oak Drive hark back to an almost forgotten age.

The early 1930s was a strange time for the movie business. The first "talkie" had heralded the end of the silent-movie era; studies were flummoxed as to how they should handle a crop of suddenly defunct actors who couldn't deliver a spoken line. Ramon Novarro was one of the relatively few exceptions. After starring in *Ben-Hur* (the 1925 film that helped establish MGM as the greatest movie studio of all) the dashing young actor became one of the world's best-known stars.

In the spring of 1930, Novarro had just taken home a healthy $125,000. But when his payment for a new car was

declined he made a devastating discovery: his assistant (and intimate companion) Louis Samuel had been embezzling his cash. One of the era's biggest screen stars was left with an account balance of just $160.

But just as the great walls of the studio backlots ensured secrecy for the movie magic conjured within, old Hollywood also protected its stars from scandal wherever possible. Novarro kept the betrayal quiet, covering his losses by repossessing the home he had recently commissioned for Samuel, designed by Lloyd Wright (son of Frank).

The palatial Samuel-Novarro house watches over the Hollywood Hills and stands as one of the city's longest-surviving masterpieces of art deco design. The exotic white-and-turquoise exterior is rich with Mayan influences while the lush interiors were assembled by MGM art director Cedric Gibbons, who filled the home with curiosities courtesy of luxury department store Bullocks Wilshire (another art deco marvel, still standing on Wilshire Boulevard).

Much of Los Angeles was built for one purpose: to be seen. It's a voyeuristic kingdom built upon an industry of watching and that's a sentiment reflected in its palaces, from the cave-like Sheats-Goldstein Residence with its dramatic triangular concrete roof to Frank Lloyd Wright's Storer House and its bizarre temple-like textile blocks.

Then there are the less obvious homes: small, quaint and swimming against the

tide of what Hollywood tells us it's all about. The one-bedroom mid-century Studio City house where Rock Hudson was photographed for *Architectural Digest* might not match the splashy celebrity we imagine, nor might Lizabeth Scott's secluded home towards the winding peak of Hollywood Boulevard.

Bounding down the path to meet me, Scott was as blonde as she had been in her final starring role in the 1950s (opposite Elvis Presley) and remained – quite literally – on top of Hollywood. Her house, designed by Robert Byrd in 1940, still exists as a landmark of elegant and timeless design, with panoramic views of the downtown district, the Paramount Pictures backlot (the backdrop to Norma Desmond's unexpected visit to Cecil B DeMille in *Sunset Boulevard*) and the neighbouring Hollywood Forever Cemetery.

Scott – who passed away in early 2015 – showed through her welcoming home that the life she lived beyond the screen had nothing in common with characters such as the reclusive Norma Desmond eternalised in the classic movie. Yet both Scott and Ramon Novarro came from a generation that valued the power of mystery, and their homes – standing tall as ever – continue to reflect that sensibility. — (M)

ABOUT THE WRITER: Ben Rylan is a producer for Monocle 24 and presenter of the weekly film culture programme *The Cinema Show*. He once narrowly avoided trouble after accidentally touching the piano from *Casablanca* at the Warner Bros studio lot.

Palm reading
The future of LA's trees

Almost everywhere you look in Los Angeles, you'll see the soaring palms that have become synonymous with the city. But could the days of this iconic tree be numbered?

by Josh Fehnert, Monocle

Los Angeles is a city of transplants, immigrants and uprooted visitors. The boulevards of this West Coast oasis have long lured fame-hungry fortune seekers, itinerant workers and émigrés – the peripatetic and the ambitious. It's when you look up, though, that you'll glimpse some of the city's most distinctive and ubiquitous imports: LA's oh-so-iconic palm trees.

In fact, only one species of these arboreal beauties is actually native to Southern California: the *Washingtonia filifera* or California palm, distinctive for the brown petticoat of dead fronds that rests, skirt-like, beneath its canopy. As for the other species of rangy evergreens, like many who call Los Angeles home, they too have an interesting tale to tell.

The first non-native palms arrived in this semi-arid patch from the Canary Islands and Mexico. They came as seeds, carried in the cassock pockets of early Franciscan preachers; 18th-century missionaries favoured the palm tree for its Biblical associations. Before long the Victorians arrived, fresh from exploring the edges of the known world and keen to plant and admire more palms as decorative mementos of their travels, symbols of their obsession with all things eastern. By the early 20th century the number of Middle Eastern date palms, Mexican fan palms and queen palms from Brazil and Bolivia had rocketed.

In the 1930s the city's first forestry commission – headed by L Glenn Hall – settled on the palm as its tree of choice for beautifying the city before the 1932 Olympics. The decision was partly motivated by thrift (at the time palms cost just $3.60 to plant, much less than magnolias) and partly as a Depression-era plan to deal with joblessness by creating a massive, decade-long public work scheme of planting.

During the 1930s some 40,000 trees were set along the city's boulevards at regular intervals of 12 to 16 metres apart. Many of them still sway in the breeze today.

As the palm gained favour on the Pacific coast its use in advertising, etchings, posters and books grew too. From postcards and restaurant names to signs and logos, this most iconic of trees began to enter the public consciousness as synonymous with Los Angeles itself.

It was, however, LA's cultural clout as the centre of a booming film industry in the middle of the 20th century that proved decisive in immortalising the palm. In images beamed around the world these silent extras hinted at the glamour and promise of Hollywood – the freedom and fun of this hedonistic hub.

"But like the plot of any decent Hollywood film, it's not necessarily smooth sailing for our planted protagonist. There's trouble brewing for LA's totemic trees"

But like the plot of any decent Hollywood film, it's not necessarily smooth sailing for our planted protagonist. There's trouble brewing for LA's totemic trees. For a start, many of the palms planted in the 1930s are now nearing the end of their natural life spans. The unsuitability of this iconic interloper is starting to show: California's water table has dropped and droughts are becoming more frequent, meaning the non-native palms are finding it tougher to survive.

People have even started moaning about the palm's civic uselessness – after all, these fruitless trees provide precious little shade for walkers. What's more, an outbreak of fungal disease and the fact that there are a few too many tree-munching red weevils on the loose have made the future of LA's palms look bleak.

In 2006 the threat was further compounded when city councillors took the decision not to replace any palms that died. Instead, the Los Angeles Department of Water and Power opted to plant 60 varieties of less thirsty, native species such as oaks and sycamores to act as replacements.

Today, aspirational builders and developers still see tall rows of palms as an Angeleno's birthright.

Other top trees

01 **El Pino**
As seen in gang film *Blood In, Blood Out* this tree in Boyle Heights has become an unlikely pilgrimage destination.

02 **Miramar Moreton Bay Fig**
Legend has it the huge tree outside the Fairmont Miramar was given by an Australian to pay his bar bill.

They're planted in driveways and frame offices; they run the lengths of boulevards from Sunset to Santa Monica and Canon Drive to Beverly Hills. The palm remains a symbol of excitement and exoticism, prosperity and leisure – even though its days are numbered.

The Los Angeles of 150 years ago was defined by forests of clumpy pepper trees, scrubland or willows; it's safe to say that the city of the future will have substantially fewer palms and more oaks and sycamores to its name. But the palm is still a potent symbol – an emblem of this enigmatic and alluring city. If nothing else it's a reminder that success, failure and intrigue are firmly rooted in almost any tale about Los Angeles. — (M)

ESSAY 03
Members of the board
Skate culture and shoes

———

When skateboarders adopted Vans as their shoes of choice, the footwear company became deeply involved in a growing culture that would define a decade in LA.

by Steve Van Doren, vice president, Vans shoes

My father worked for a shoe company in Boston for 20 years before they moved him to California. One day, at a surfing event at Huntington Beach, he met legendary surfer Duke Kahanamoku and that same day decided to make a pair of shoes out of his shirt – it was a blue Hawaiian number. Two months later he quit his job to fulfil his dream of making his own shoes in his own factory. Together with my Uncle Jim and a third person called Gordon Lee, he founded Vans in Anaheim in 1966.

My brothers and sisters and I have been involved in the company from the early days; I was a talker so my job was passing flyers door to door. When my father would open a shop, I'd be there. My mother was the first shop manager and then a friend's wife was the next. Every shop he'd open I'd be there, at 10 or 11 years old, selling shoes.

When my father made shoes for Vans they had to be better than his competitors'

ABOUT THE WRITER: Josh Fehnert is MONOCLE's Edits Editor (and a budding amateur botanist) who first visited LA in 2008. Griffith Park is his favourite place to take in the city's fine native foliage and dusty hills.

because nobody knew the brand. Back then he made the sole twice as thick as PF Flyers, Keds or Converse. He used thick, 10-ounce (283g) duck canvas and nylon thread. Everything was reinforced. So when someone bought a pair of shoes, it would last.

After a couple of years Vans were adopted by skateboarders who decided they liked the shoe – the grip of the sole, the durability and the fit. We would do things that other companies wouldn't: if someone wore a size eight on one foot and seven on the other, we'd sell them one of each.

In the mid 1970s, Stacy Peralta, Tony Alva and Jay Adams – skateboarders known as the "Dogtown" guys – would go to our shops in Venice or Santa Monica because they had worn out one shoe from using that foot to brake. In those days a pair of Vans cost about $7 so we'd sell them one shoe for $3.50. One day Alva – who had a navy pair – decided he wanted one in red even though the other foot would be in navy. Eventually we just started giving them shoes. They would come in, get their free shoes, wear them for a couple of weeks and then come back for more – they became our guinea pigs.

We came out with our first skate shoe in 1976 and that's when our slogan "Off The Wall" was born. There had been a drought and pools across the city had to be emptied. Alva and the others would jump fences, pump out the last 50 gallons (190ltr) or so and then skate in the pools – literally coming off the wall.

My dad knew nothing about skateboarding but we saw what they were doing and we backed them 100 per cent. We did everything we could and scraped

> *"We would do things that other companies wouldn't: if someone wore a size eight on one foot and seven on the other, we'd sell them one of each"*

together whatever money we had in order to sponsor them. They were always loyal to us and we hired our first skate manager in 1977.

At first we made canvas shoes, then the skaters asked for some leather to make them last longer. That became the Style 36 with the side strip. From the outset my father made custom shoes. The skaters wanted to be different and we did whatever they asked. A custom shoe cost them just 50 cents more back in the day.

Skaters are individuals; they didn't want to be part of a team. They were great athletes but they had this attitude that suggested, "I do what I want to do". We were the small guys – the company that no one knew – and they were our cast of pirates and outcasts with their spiked hair, tattoos and piercings. We backed them and put their pictures in magazines.

We put shoes on individuals who went on to become stars: they became their own folk heroes. They had the driving force to go out and do what people said not to. That was their spirit; they were off the wall. — (M)

ABOUT THE WRITER: Steve Van Doren is the son of Vans co-founder, Paul Van Doren. He started working for the family business aged 10 and today serves as the vice-president of events and promotions, as well as Vans's unofficial "ambassador of fun".

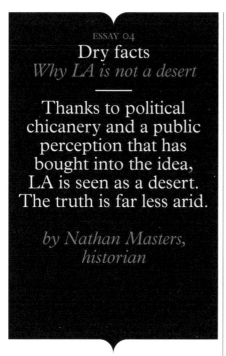

ESSAY 04
Dry facts
Why LA is not a desert
────

Thanks to political chicanery and a public perception that has bought into the idea, LA is seen as a desert. The truth is far less arid.

by Nathan Masters, historian

"Scratch the surface a little and the desert shows through." Bertolt Brecht was commenting as much on the city's cultural landscape as its physical topography when he penned those words about Los Angeles in 1941. But in grasping for a metaphor for LA's then cultural shallowness, the German intellectual seized on a pervasive and persistent fallacy about the city: that it's a natural desert.

He has plenty of company. Jack Kerouac's *On the Road* (1957) described Los Angeles as a "huge desert encampment". Evelyn Waugh opened a 1947 *Life* article with a fanciful vision of the future: "Bel-Air and Beverly Hills will lie naked save for scrub and cactus…

while the horned toad and the turkey buzzard leave their faint imprint on the dunes that will drift on Sunset Boulevard." The notion continues to pollute private conversation and public discourse. The *Los Angeles Times* called a 2003 editorial on the city's water policy "It's Still a Desert". In fact, it isn't – and it never has been.

LA poorly fits almost all scientific understandings of the term "desert", most of which describe a region where evapotranspiration outpaces precipitation, desiccating the land, forcing plant and animal life to adapt to the extreme conditions. Quite simply, Los Angeles gets too much rain to qualify: an average of 15 inches (38.1cm) per year, well above the 10-inch (25.4cm) upper limit for a desert at this latitude. The standard Köppen classification system places LA's Mediterranean climate of warm, dry summers and cool, wet winters within the same category as Athens and Seville – places few would call deserts.

True desert settlements lie just over the mountain ranges that shield LA from North America's harsh continental air

> *"Los Angeles simply gets too much rain: an average of 15 inches per year, well above the 10-inch upper limit for a desert at this latitude"*

**It never rains
but it pours**
——
01 **Flood of 1938**
Freakishly high rainfall led to
more than 100 deaths as large
parts of LA were inundated.
02 **Flood of 2005**
LA's highest levels of rain since
the 1880s led to metre-high
floods, collapsed bridges and
caused rockslides.

masses. Las Vegas gets 4.2 inches (10.68cm) of rain per year and Yuma just 3.3 (8.38cm). But on the cooler Los Angeles side of the mountains, maritime influences prevail. Fog blankets the coastal plain with some regularity. "June Gloom" dampens the spirits of Angelenos at the start of every summer.

Quibble over the meaning of "desert" if you like; it has certainly shifted over the centuries. But the earliest written descriptions of the Los Angeles area also reveal a landscape that resists any sober definition of the word.

In the summer of 1769 an expedition of Spanish soldiers and missionaries encountered "a very spacious valley, well grown with cottonwoods and alders, among which ran a beautiful river." The expedition's diarist Juan Crespí noted that "all the soil is black and loamy and is capable of producing every kind of grain and fruit which may be planted."

Seven years later another party of explorers visited the site. "The land was very green and flowery," missionary Pedro Font said, "with a great deal of miry grounds created by the rains."

In 1781, 44 Mexican settlers trekked north from Sonora and Sinaloa and founded an agricultural village on the spot. For well over a century, local streams and aquifers quenched the thirst of "El Pueblo de la Reina de los Angeles", even as it grew into a US city.

If Los Angeles was once so wet how did anyone ever mistake it for desert? We can blame urban development for literally covering up the evidence. Wetlands are now leafy suburbs and willow-lined creeks concrete storm sewers. A century's worth of utopian thinking about Los Angeles, which casts its past and natural environment as little more than a blank slate, also bears some responsibility. So does the nagging suspicion that the city's very existence is a crime against nature (see Brecht, Waugh et al).

Most of all you can blame the architects of LA's modern water infrastructure. In 1904 a sceptical electorate stood in the way of William Mulholland's audacious proposal to tap the eastern slope of the Sierra Nevada by way of a 233-mile (374.9km) aqueduct. So the water superintendent and his political allies exaggerated the region's aridity, falsely claiming that a 10-year drought gripped the city.

Screenwriter Robert Towne dramatised this rhetoric of aridity in the 1974 film *Chinatown*. "Los Angeles is a desert community," a mayoral figure tells a crowd inside city hall. "Beneath this building, beneath every street, there's a desert. Without this water the dust will rise up and cover us as though we'd never existed!"

Such warnings were a self-fulfilling prophecy. LA convinced itself it was a desert, diverted rivers from distant watersheds and engineered a flood-control system that flushes local rainfall to the sea – 10 billion gallons (37.85 billion litres) squandered with each passing storm. Meanwhile, it grew beyond the constraints of its local hydrology, from a population of 102,479 in 1900 to 1,238,048 in 1930.

There's no denying LA's semi-aridity or that weather is highly variable from year to year and subject to longer cycles. The next drought is never far away – and anthropogenic climate change means it might be longer and more severe than the last. But precisely because water is so precious Los Angeles must adopt a more nuanced understanding of its natural climate, one that takes its local water supply seriously. Then perhaps we can stop talking about that sinister, dubious desert lurking beneath. — (M)

ABOUT THE WRITER: Nathan Masters writes about Los Angeles history. He hosts and produces *Lost LA*, a public television series from KCET and the USC Libraries.

ESSAY 05
Where the art is
LA: cultural hub

___

With its high concentration of creatives, is it any wonder that Los Angeles has become a destination for galleries and lovers of contemporary art?

by Marie-Sophie Schwarzer, Monocle

By the time Los Angeles was founded on 4 September 1781, the Old World had already witnessed the creation of countless masterpieces by maestros from Leonardo da Vinci to Rembrandt. In contrast, LA's native Yang-na tribe left no legacy of artistry or even pottery-making behind. It was a culturally barren land. But this simply made the city a blank slate, one that inspired generations to invest in bringing culture to its shores.

Today's LA is the creative capital of the US. There are more artists, actors, writers, film-makers and musicians living and working in LA than any other city in the country. And with more than 800 art galleries and museums, its cultural wealth – even beyond Hollywood – generates some 640,000 jobs and more than $200bn in revenue.

The city may never acquire the sweeping collections of historic art that London, Paris and New York possess but this dearth of the classics has also focused the young city on the "now" – as a prime market for contemporary art. LA is home to the legendary Moca (*see page 95*) – the city's first museum dedicated to contemporary art, founded in 1979 – and a wealth of art schools.

Add to this the fact that the US occupies a leading position in the art sphere, with a growing global market share value of 43 per cent (streets ahead of its runner-up, the UK), and it was only a matter of time before the world's leading galleries came flocking to this corner of the globe. It was LA's potential and undeniable pool of artistic talent that finally encouraged international galleries such as Berlin's Sprüth Magers and Zürich's Hauser & Wirth to come to the city.

"Los Angeles has always been a special place for Manuela and me since we first visited in the late 1980s," says Iwan Wirth, who opened the sixth branch of Hauser & Wirth (*see page 99*) with his wife and Paul Schimmel in a former flour mill in the booming Arts District 24 years after founding the original gallery in Switzerland. "Opening a space here was never a matter of if, only when."

Over the past few years more than 50 galleries have set up shop in LA and the city also got its first critical arts journal *The Contemporary Art Review LA*, which launched in 2015. "Los Angeles is one of four cultural capitals of the world, along with New York, London and Paris," says Eli Broad, the godfather of the city's art scene and founder of The Broad (*see page 93*) which houses his star-studded 2,000-piece art collection. "We are also now the contemporary-art capital."

Slowly but surely the home of the Art Los Angeles Contemporary fair has become an autonomous arts centre with its heart in Downtown LA. The lofty

"With more than 800 art galleries and museums, LA's cultural wealth generates some 640,000 jobs and more than $200bn in revenue"

Must-see art

01 'Urban Light', Chris Burden
This installation outside Lacma uses 202 vintage street lamps
02 'Irises', Van Gogh
The artist's 1889 painting hangs at the Getty Center.
03 'The Great Wave off Kanagawa', Hokusai
The woodblock print is at the Hammer Museum.

warehouses and gritty, graffitied streets of the Arts District and neighbouring Boyle Heights were once home to artists from Constance Mallinson to Paul McCarthy; today they attract craft breweries, coffee roasteries and galleries such as New York's Maccarone.

Just two years ago well-known LA-based artists such as Mark Bradford, Sterling Ruby, John Baldessari, Barbara Kruger and Liza Lou didn't have galleries here. Now incoming institutions are vying to sign up the city's talent. Subsequently LA's presence in the art market is being felt more than ever and the opening of The Broad and the $602m Peter Zumthor expansion of Miracle Mile's Lacma (*see page 95*) are securing its position in the future.

"Los Angeles rewards curiosity, a sense of adventure and freedom for those who search off the beaten path," says Wirth. "That spirit is now rewarded by the sheer density of cultural destinations here. The city's institutions reflect a homegrown cosmopolitanism, something that has always been unique to LA but perhaps not always celebrated as it is now." And yet the cultural party, it seems, has only just begun. — (M)

ABOUT THE WRITER: Growing up watching *Pretty Woman*, MONOCLE writer Marie-Sophie Schwarzer has always had a soft spot for LA. On her latest trip, reporting for this guide, it was the museums and galleries that enchanted her.

ESSAY 06

The reel thing
LA's indie movie scene

For most, movies in Los Angeles are all about Hollywood blockbusters. But the vibrant and edgy independent film-making community is where the real innovation lies.

*by Josh Welsh,
president of Film
Independent*

Growing up in Washington in the 1970s and 1980s, "California" was tossed around as a casual insult. This may seem mystifying today but back then it resonated – at least in my family. My mother's scorn for the Golden State was the most intense, so when my sister chose to go to the University of California all my mother could do was shake her head and give her most withering put-down ("What a bunch of big, fat nothings"), followed by an angry exhalation of cigarette smoke.

The anti-California stance wasn't unique to my mother. When I decided to move to Los Angeles from Baltimore in the late 1990s my friends were genuinely distressed for me. I'd hear "God, I'm so sorry you have to move there", as if going from Baltimore to LA was some sort of tragic step-down. I loved Baltimore – full of misfits, dreamers, artists and weirdos – but was pretty sure a move to the sunny West Coast wasn't so bad.

I arrived with a headful of clichés about the city. Overwhelmed by the sheer size and sprawl of the place I first orientated myself by seeking out places I knew (or thought I knew) from movies and TV: Hollywood Boulevard, Rodeo Drive, Malibu et al – iconic places I had to see, based on the countless films I'd been raised on.

After the initial rush that came with discovering that so many of the clichés were true, or true enough, I realised that LA was an amorphous sprawl that contained just as many weirdos as Baltimore – except many of them were waggling video cameras.

While I was prepared for the outsized influence of "Hollywood" I was quickly and pleasantly surprised by the number of talented independent film-makers here. By luck, I stumbled across Film Independent,

"The fact is that Los Angeles is what New York usually gets all the credit for being: the true birthplace of independent cinema"

then known as IFP/West, an organisation that serves independent film-makers, producing the LA Film Festival and the Independent Spirit Awards, among many other things. In short order I became a member and then a volunteer (my first event: working a screening of Todd Solondz's *Welcome to the Dollhouse*).

The fact is that LA is what New York usually gets all the credit for being: the true birthplace of independent cinema. From John Cassavetes making films out of his home in the Hollywood Hills to David Lynch shooting *Eraserhead* while finishing film school at the American Film Institute, this is where independent, artist-driven film-making has flourished.

While the big studios continue to make fewer (and bigger) films each year, great independent film continues to come out of Los Angeles: Sean Baker's *Tangerine*, a sweetly comedic film about the Santa Monica Boulevard of transgender sex workers and doughnut shops, is a take on the city that you'd never see in bigger-budget fare – but one you will see if you get out of your car and explore the streets of LA. Or Ava DuVernay's *Middle of Nowhere*, the story of a woman whose husband is serving an eight-year prison sentence, which gives us a window on life in Compton, a world that bears little resemblance to the gang stories Hollywood regularly churns out. And then there's Jill Soloway's *Afternoon Delight*, about a stay-at-

Three LA indies

01 **500 Days of Summer**
Smitten Tom takes girlfriend Summer to his top LA haunts.
02 **The Informers**
LA's excesses in the 1980s are examined in this Bret Easton Ellis adaptation.
03 **Killer of Sheep**
Haunting 1978 drama set in LA's Watts district.

home Silver Lake mother who invites a stripper to become her live-in nanny, a finely observed film that captures the world of young, well-educated eastside parents grappling with adult responsibilities.

When I didn't move back to Baltimore some of my friends said disapprovingly, "Oh, you've been seduced". Maybe so but not by the weather or any of those "iconic places" I first visited. If there's one film that captures my love for LA it's David Lynch's *Mulholland Drive*. Ostensibly the story of aspiring actress Betty, who has just moved to LA, and Rita, an amnesiac woman she befriends, it's a tour de force meditation on LA and its mythologies. It's a flick that rewards frequent viewings. Every time I watch it I find myself asking, "Wait, why exactly did I come here?" And before I've even finished that train of thought, I'm answering: "But there's no place I'd rather be". — (M)

ABOUT THE WRITER: Josh Welsh is the president of Film Independent, the organisation that produces the Film Independent Spirit Awards, the LA Film Festival and Film Independent at Los Angeles County Museum of Art.

ESSAY 07

Driven to distraction
The cult of the car

———

The City of Angels is also the City of Autos, with the car worshipped so devoutly that everything from pop culture to architecture has adapted accordingly.

*by Ed Stocker,
Monocle*

**LA's most
congested freeways**
———

01 Southbound 101
Between Topanga Canyon
Boulevard and Vignes Street.
02 The 5 Freeway
Highway 133 Orange County
to Olympic Boulevard.
03 The 10 Freeway
Between Santa Monica and
Alameda Street.

Like many New World cities Los Angeles hasn't always valued its heritage, tearing down buildings to placate the dual totems of profitability and progress. Nowadays, though, that ethos of constant renewal is being rethought as the city considers its legacy. Yet finding something old and smoothed by years of wear can be difficult.

That's why a visit to the beautiful Moorish-influenced San Gabriel Arcángel, built by Spanish colonists in the 1770s, is essential. Researching this book, I headed to its sleepy eastern neighbourhood with the single goal of admiring its shingled roof and buttressed walls. Then I spotted a poster in front of the venerable building announcing a festival: Mission San Gabriel Blessing of the Cars (free parking, naturally). I'd realised that this was a city obsessed with the automobile but I hadn't quite grasped how far the fixation extended – to members of the Catholic clergy laying hands on a stream of gas-guzzlers.

LA isn't alone in its auto-mania. US popular culture is steeped in the deification of the car, from the ubiquitous drive-thrus to countless scenes of drive-in movies that pepper Hollywood's back-catalogue. But nowhere is it taken to such epic and extreme measures as here.

Driving in LA can be petrifying, especially if you're the timid, no-I-insist-after-you type of driver that I am. You soon learn that, unlike Europe (and probably Canada), lane differentiations don't exist. If you think of traffic as swarming hornets, weaving in and out of lanes and probably not signalling while doing it, you come some way to understanding how it feels.

But then after a few days something shifted in my consciousness: I began to enjoy it. Despite the terrible drivers and the irredeemable damage I was doing to the environment, I revelled – selfishly, perhaps – in the personal space I had to navigate the city (and with a great soundtrack to boot). Because despite the freeways there are also iconic avenues to cruise, as well as the dreamy Pacific Coast Highway snaking north to Malibu.

One of the most fascinating aspects of LA car culture is the way in which the metropolis has been shaped by it architecturally. Brands, advertisers, restaurants and shops have all had to try to appeal to the motorist speeding past – and that has meant employing every trick in the book. Nowadays this may mean towering signs and flashing lights but LA's rich legacy in this field is worth considering.

"US popular culture is steeped in the deification of the car but nowhere is it taken to such epic and extreme measures as here"

Googie architecture is a fine example: a mid-century offshoot that was inspired by progress, space travel and a world of seemingly endless possibility. Buildings were designed colourfully, with plenty of glass, but it was the jagged roofs and soaring, spiky signage that was there to arouse the intrigue of drivers. Perhaps the weirdest and most wonderful of them all, however, was another all-but-dead art form: programmatic architecture. The aim? Create a building in the shape of the product that is being sold inside it. One excellent example of this was The Tamale, a "Spanish delights" restaurant that opened in 1928 and was shaped – you guessed it – like a giant, wrapped tamale. Today the structure still exists although it now functions as a beauty salon. There are other buildings worth tracking down too, from The Donut Hole in La Puente to former camera shop The Darkroom in the Miracle Mile area.

Los Angeles has evolved of course, and it continues to do so. Googie and programmatic architecture have had their day and there are finally signs that the city is losing its blind faith in motoring. As public-transport links continue to be developed, let's hope that the city comes up with innovative and aesthetic ways to appeal to these new travellers. LA has its legacy to think about, remember. — (M)

ABOUT THE WRITER: Ed Stocker is MONOCLE's New York bureau chief and has overseen the New York and Miami books in our travel guide series. He's a big fan of the city hiking and endless taco opportunities of LA – and is trying his best to become an aggressive driver.

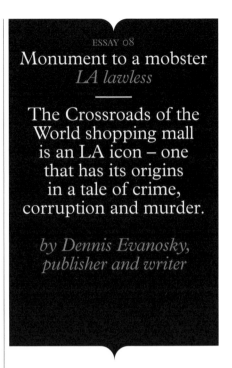

ESSAY 08

Monument to a mobster
LA lawless

The Crossroads of the World shopping mall is an LA icon – one that has its origins in a tale of crime, corruption and murder.

by Dennis Evanosky, publisher and writer

Most will instantly recognise the Crossroads of the World on Sunset Boulevard, with its soaring tower, revolving globe and portholes that make it look like an ocean liner. But many are unaware that Ella Crawford conceived it as a shopping mall to erase the memory of her husband's murder: renowned mobster Charles "Good Time Charlie" Crawford lost his life here in 1931. He was shot dead – along with friend and former police reporter Herbert Spencer – by David "Debonair Dave" Clark in a small office building that once stood on the same spot.

On May 20, so the story goes, Charles was sitting in his property agency with Spencer when

"Parrot and Charles pulled the strings while puppet-mayor George E Cryer danced. Effectively they ran the city"

Debonair Dave stepped across the threshold and gunned them down. Not long after, Clark confessed to the murders claiming self-defence. A brazen admission considering investigators discovered that neither victim was armed and Spencer had taken a bullet to the heart. Spencer was collateral damage, the rumour mill suggested. Tongues wagged around town, intimating that Charles's murder was a hit, paid for by one of his enemies; quite possibly gambling kingpin Guy McAfee.

Charles was born in Youngstown, Ohio, in 1879. The Klondike Gold Rush had lured him west and he was in his early twenties when he decided that living outside the law suited him rather well. He made a tidy sum mining the miners in Seattle, his prostitutes and "barmaids" filching gold from their pockets at dance halls he owned until the mayor's frequent visits to these dens cost him his job.

The ensuing scandal caused Charles to flee and he followed the crowds (and the criminals) to LA, attracted by the money and power that comes with an oil boom and a blossoming movie industry. Here, Charles opened the Maple Bar at Fifth and Maple and set up a ruthless crime syndicate, The City Hall Gang. From 1921 to 1929 he and political fixer Kent Kane Parrot pulled the strings while puppet-mayor George E Cryer danced. Effectively Parrot and Charles ran the city.

Parrot's power extended past the mayor's office to the Harbor Commission and the police force. Charles looked over Parrot's shoulder as he manipulated officers without ever consulting the parade of police chiefs throughout the 1920s.

It's no wonder that Charles ruffled a few feathers along the way: he no doubt incured the wrath of Guy McAfee but "Handsome Johnny" Roselli, Jack Dragna and any number of others could have sent Debonair Dave to take him out.

Clark got away with the murders. The first trial ended in a hung jury (the lone holdout for a guilty verdict found a bomb on his doorstep). Nobody was

LA's most notorious gangsters
—
01 Vito Di Giorgio
Shot dead while getting a shave and a haircut.
02 Joseph Ardizzone
The only LA mobster reputedly killed by his own men.
03 Rosario DeSimone
Crime boss to all of Los Angeles County.

surprised when the jury in the retrial found Clark not guilty.

Ella recovered remarkably quickly and had soon arranged a second marriage; she had two daughters to support after all. She met C Roy Smith in September 1931 and they married just a few months later in Yuma, Arizona. That same year she demolished the fated property-agency building and hired architect Robert V Derrah to replace 6665 Sunset Boulevard with something more positive: cue Crossroads of the World.

Ella and Smith divorced in 1934 and she pined for Charles, reclaiming his name. Clark went free and killed again; on Armistice Day 1953 he murdered his friend's wife, "Toots" Blair. He was sentenced to five years to life in Chino State Prison but just a few weeks into his sentence succumbed to a brain haemorrhage.

Ella passed away in 1953, closing one of the more bizarre chapters in LA's history. If you wander through Crossroads today, listen carefully; some say "Good Time Charlie" and his Ella still haunt the place. But be careful – you just might run into Debonair Dave. — (M)

ABOUT THE WRITER: Dennis Evanosky co-publishes the *Alameda Sun* newspaper. He has 10 books to his credit, including two about Los Angeles.

ESSAY 09
Get out of town
Desert living

———

The mad pace of city living is not for everyone, and life in the desert outside LA can have a magnetism that's impossible to resist – or even define.

by Lily Stockman, artist

The drive home looks like this: as you head north on Old Woman Springs Road the geological scramble collapses into a black basalt expanse called Flamingo Heights. The desert runs amok with Joshua trees, Spanish dagger yuccas, pink barrel cacti and golden chollas that catch the light like rearview-mirror disco balls. A beyond-place. Home.

The first time I moved from New York to Joshua Tree (about two hours east of LA by car) was eight years ago, by order of the US Marine Corps – my husband was to be stationed at the desert base of Twentynine Palms. We were young newlyweds, me a jock-turned-art-school kid and he a post-September 11 idealist with good intentions and a great Physical Fitness Test score.

We found a house by the entrance to Joshua Tree National Park, bought a Tacoma pick-up and got a mutt from the pound – the Joshua Tree starter kit. We were joining the fray of "childless hippies with lawn ornaments made from old cars",

Desert attractions
—
01 Borrego Springs
Surrounded by state park, this
town has epic stargazing.
02 Salton Sea
Find these spooky abandoned
beaches four hours from LA.
03 The Integratron
A meditation site in Landers,
built to contact aliens.
No, really.

as one New Yorker friend bluntly put it.

I rented an unplumbed shed downtown for my studio and my husband trained to be an infantry officer in the hot scrub before shipping out to a different desert. In those seven months alone I occupied myself the way people do in the desert: I read, hiked, painted – a life wholly self-directed, not by choice but by necessity. My loneliness in those first months evolved into a comfortable solitude. I learned how to be alone; it was the happiest unhappy time of my life. And when my husband returned safely from war it was blissful.

Then we left. My husband got out of the Marines and we moved to India for a year. We returned to graduate school, pursued teaching fellowships, chipped away at student debt and participated in early-thirties anxiety about where and how to live. Urban or rural? Corporate or self-employment? Health benefits or time and space benefits? All our conversations pointed back to the desert. Home.

We longed for desert life and missed our friends, people who taught us to read the orographic lift of clouds off the Sawtooth Mountains and how to fix a swamp cooler. Independent people who relied on each other. It surprised me that I was nostalgic for the sense of being on the brink of my adult life that I experienced when my husband left for Iraq. He missed the quiet, the tight-knit community and a plot of land to steward. So we trawled online for cabins. After three years, we found an asbestos-shingled cabin with water and power. It's the colour of poached salmon – and for now it's part-time home.

Things have changed in the years we've been gone. There are more people; a barely perceptible glow of light pollution from new big-box shops in Yucca Valley fuzzes the horizon as we watch on hot summer nights for shooting stars. There is more traffic, more people seeking solitude and space in the desert. And who can blame them? We came back for the same.

The word nostalgia comes from the Latinised Greek *nostos* ("return home") and *algos* ("pain"). The homeward journey in classical epics is always tinged with a slight sadness and our homecoming is no exception. But the heart of my *algos* lies in my own relationship to the place: I thought coming back to Joshua Tree would be the salve, the answer to my anxieties about how, where and why to live life a certain way. I realise there's a younger version of myself that stayed behind in the boulders by the Park those eight years ago and that my adult self is a little more world-weary, a little less optimistic.

My husband and I meet up with friends for an evening hike to look for petroglyphs. Halfway up the canyon we run into an ornithologist who tells us a pair of golden eagles is nesting up on the mesa. "First time in years," he says, beaming. The late light casts the rabbitbrush in halos of gold and the monzonite canyon walls glow apricot. "Not a bad place to call home," he says, taking in the sublime gloaming, before continuing down the trail. — (M)

> *"My loneliness in those first months evolved to a comfortable solitude. I learned how to be alone; it was the happiest unhappy time of my life"*

ABOUT THE WRITER: Lily Stockman is a painter. She splits her time between Los Angeles, Joshua Tree and Jaipur, where she runs Block Shop Textiles with her sister, textile designer Hopie Stockman.

ESSAY 10

Evolution of a neighbourhood
The Arts District

The changes to LA's Arts District range from subtle to sweeping. Has the spirit of this creative enclave survived?

by Melissa Richardson Banks, photographer and writer

"*Just over a decade ago, nearly 1,500 artists resided here in 35 buildings. Today, there are more than 6,000 people here and fewer than 100 are artists*"

I moved to Downtown Los Angeles from Texas in 1993, settling in the Arts District almost immediately after visiting the area. Back then to get into the artist-in-residence lofts you had to be a working artist and at the time, I wasn't, but I did eventually become one. In retrospect perhaps my initial entrance to the Arts District as a non-artist resident was the first crack in the dam through which changes now flood into the community.

The history of the Arts District has been one of constant flux and reinvention: there have been many endings and many beginnings over the course of nearly two centuries. The area was once full of vineyards and citrus groves, before it became a working-class neighbourhood that was then soon replaced by a thriving manufacturing industry. Abandoned factories were later transformed by artists into studios. Fast forward to the present day and the area has become a popular destination for those looking to eat, drink and explore.

As a small-town girl who grew up sweeping metal shavings off the floor of my father's machine shop, the Arts District immediately felt like home. Back then it was an industrial yet surprisingly peaceful oasis in the middle of an overwhelmingly large city. Very few lived Downtown at the time and the thousands who worked there daily rarely stayed after dark.

When meandering through today's bustling Arts District it's hard to believe that just over a decade ago nearly 1,500 artists resided here in roughly 35 historic loft buildings that sprawled over 52 blocks (today, there are more than 6,000 people here and fewer than 100 are artists). To outsiders the gritty industrial area appeared to be uninhabited and was filled with ugly nondescript commercial structures, often with graffiti-tagged walls that belied their inner architectural beauty. Determined to get somewhere else drivers would speed along Santa Fe Avenue, which connected two freeways without a single stop sign or signal for well over a mile; a stark contrast to today, with drivers circling the streets like vultures eyeing their prey, hoping for that rare parking spot to become available.

For years there were only a handful of shops, bars, restaurants and galleries. The heart of the Arts District was at 3rd and Traction, where most artists congregated, day and night. Community activist Joel Bloom was our de facto mayor for years, and his bellowing voice either welcomed or frightened you when entering his tiny corner shop at Traction and Hewitt. Bloom's General Store was stocked with a hodgepodge of art magazines, cigars hidden from view under the counter, videos (and later DVDs) and dog treats.

Arts District murals
—
01 **'Decaying Sea-Lion'**
By Belgian artist ROA, at the junction of Jesse and Imperial.
02 **'Wrinkles in the City'**
On the side of Angel City Brewery; it's by JR from France.
03 **'Community Wall'**
At the corner of Traction Avenue and Hewitt; it's where anyone can paint.

Next door to Bloom's was Soul Folks Café (now The Pie Hole), which locals nicknamed "Slow Folks" due to the speed of the service. Yet it endured because the food was so good. Around the corner was Al's Bar, which has been closed since 2001. This infamous dive bar was where aspiring punk rock and alternative bands played during the 1980s and 1990s, some of whom – such as Red Hot Chili Peppers, Nirvana and Beck – went on to widespread fame. Upstairs, the century-old American Hotel provided affordable single rooms that artists and musicians could stay in for a week or a month. Some stayed for years and, even now, with its recent purchase by a developer, there are still a few old-timers who have lived there since the 1980s.

While street art, graffiti tags and crew mural collaborations were evident in earlier years, a series of large-scale murals by local and international artists soon became the norm in the Arts District during the few years prior to the blockbuster *Art in the Streets* exhibition at The Geffen Contemporary at Moca in 2011. At their high point between 2009 and 2013 there were more than 150 new murals in the neighbourhood; most were organised by LA Freewalls.

In 2010 I started to notice changes in my adopted neighbourhood and began taking photographs: first a shot or two every other day, then a daily deluge of images, documenting the transformation as the pace accelerated. Art was pasted and painted everywhere but there were other structural changes: a sausage-and-beer establishment replaced a former printing company and attracted visitors from far away; and a grungy old warehouse was slowly demolished, revealing a historical architectural structure that should have been preserved but was razed to make room for a new apartment complex.

The transformations currently happening are inevitable – and, for the most part, good news for the neighbourhood. A former flour mill was beautifully converted, maintaining its historic integrity, into the Southern California outpost of an international art gallery. We now have an immense variety of places to eat and meet people. Best of all, in spite of the explosive growth I can still walk down the street and run into neighbours I know. I have ridden the emotional waves of change and have finally found peace with it all. I embrace the present, I hope for the future and, while not dwelling on it for too long, still admit that I occasionally long for the simplicity of the past. — (M)

ABOUT THE WRITER: Melissa Richardson Banks is a photographer and writer specialising in Downtown Los Angeles, the South Bay and South Texas. She is also an independent producer of events such as community festivals, pop-up dinners and art salons.

ESSAY I I
Transports of delight
Metro art
———
A wide-reaching programme of artworks is helping to sell the idea of public transport to the notoriously car-loving Angelenos.

*by Julia Wick,
writer and editor*

A giant formation of sandy-coloured rocks juts over the entrance to the Vermont/Beverly Metro Station, towering above an escalator that appears to disappear into the darkness below. "I wanted to reveal the relationship of the subway to its geological environment," sculptor George Stone told *The New York Times* in 1998, a year before the station that bears his large-scale installation – and the second phase of Los Angeles' Red Line subway through Hollywood – opened. Stone drew on the geology of the location in designing his rock formations, creating a space that feels equal parts primordial and post-apocalyptic.

Despite the inherent singularity of a subway station styled somewhere between a disaster movie and a return-to-nature fantasy, Vermont/Beverly is unique only in the theme of its installation. Since 1989, Metro (the agency responsible for public transportation in Los Angeles) has set aside half a per cent of all construction costs for public art, making it an integral part of every rail and light-rail station. The programme was, and continues to be, hugely ambitious – not just in physical scope or the estimated total of $25 m spent on public art over the past quarter-century – but also in its dedication to creating a cultural shift in a city notoriously wed to private living and personal automobiles.

Metro Art's early aim was not just to beautify stations but also to help sell the entire concept of public transport through a new narrative rooted in place and civic identity. Today, the work of 148 artists can be seen in more than 125 stations across the vast expanse of Los Angeles. Those numbers will be even bigger years from now, when the city's rail system extends down Wilshire to Century City and through South LA to the airport.

A small miracle is usually required to create any kind of good art, let alone public art in a renascent rail system, which has to claw its way through a bureaucratic haze of proposals, budgets, politics and policy. Early on, the transit authority set out five conditions for artists: chosen works must be high quality, site-specific, expected to last at least 25 years, vandal-resistant and require minimal maintenance. Artists are selected through a peer-review process with community input and all works are created for their site. Implicit is the promise that each work will reflect or even tell the rider something about each neighbourhood and its residents. History is carved in limestone capitals set

atop two-metre-tall metal pillars (Duarte/City of Hope Station), delicately rendered through ceramic tile vignettes (Westlake/MacArthur Park Station) and ghostily echoed through a giant mural of mingling travellers from different Los Angeles eras (Union Station). At Slauson Station, the entire history of South Central Los Angeles – from prehistory to the 21st century – is compressed into 96 porcelain-enamelled steel panels, designed by a famed East LA art collective.

Over at Pershing Square Station, meanwhile, the luminous neon bursts suspended high above the tracks suggest the sultry marquees of Broadway, a block over. Passengers can catch a glimpse of the bright lights as the train car pauses briefly in the station, momentarily rooting them to something legible even as they rocket through the bowels of the city.

"Implicit is the promise that each work will reflect or even tell the rider something about each neighbourhood and its residents"

Public memory in Metro's Los Angeles is writ small and large across ceilings and walls and concrete benches. Not everyone, however, sees the charm. Reviewing the Red Line stations in Hollywood, an architecture critic derided their separateness, each with its own theme, work and creators. "It reflects a Balkanised Los Angeles – a fragmented, divided city rather than a cohesive metropolis," he wrote, somehow missing the point entirely.

Here in Los Angeles, where 72 suburbs famously went in search of a city, we take pride in our hodgepodge architectural styles, our interlocking ethnic enclaves and the infinite, exquisitely distinct identities on display throughout this very guidebook. Metro Art's unifying glue is the site-specific spectacle

Union Station art

01 'Traveler', East Entrance
Tile mural of historical travellers.
02 'La Sombra del Arroyo', MTA Transit Plaza
A faux-arboreal canopy.
03 'City of Dreams, River of History', East Lobby
Looming faces of early settlers and present-day Angelenos.

resplendent in some element of every station, each one a rallying cry against the generic city

When it opens sometime in 2019, the Crenshaw Line will run through the heart of south LA, eventually connecting the already-built Expo Line to Los Angeles International Airport. The artists for all eight of the stations have already been selected and their work is being integrated throughout the construction process. Much of the art for the line's above-ground stations will be rendered on enormous fused-glass panels (the material retains its vibrancy even under the beating sun, making it a transit-system favourite) that loom high above the tracks, visible not just to commuters but also the community at large. Because at its crux, Metro's public-art programme is about more than the aesthetic benefit of its riders. Each cultural landmark is an individual square in a much larger quilt, the fabric of a city filled with mythology. — (M)

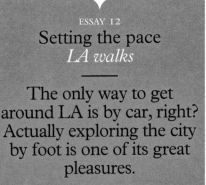

ESSAY 12

Setting the pace
LA walks

———

The only way to get around LA is by car, right? Actually exploring the city by foot is one of its great pleasures.

by Robert Bound, Monocle

Los Angeles was sketched out by the railroad companies as they pushed ever westward until they hit the surf. Steam power and rails were bad-mouthed by the machinations of a motor empire selling freedom and laying roads everywhere. And look what happened: doomed romance at every turn. The future of the motor car was 1957: chrome bumpers and sculpted steel, bench-seats, wings and one-finger-in-your-belt-loop. But now you have to take provisions and a spare phone battery just to drive across town. You're in a jam, Sam. The future got old quick.

Today I'm wearing a stout pair of Nikes to walk around LA while I tell you why, as a car-lover, the best way to transport yourself around this place is on your tootsies. I'm not talking about getting from Santa Monica to Hollywood (three hours and 26 minutes from the Pier to The Standard on Sunset, according to Google Maps) but from one neighbourhood to the next, little by little, until drivers don't think you're a hobo just because you're taking a stroll.

By the way, I was convinced of this notion last time I was in Culver City to interview Ed Ruscha, that great lion of the Los Angeles art scene. We were in

ABOUT THE WRITER: Julia Wick is a staff writer at LAist and former senior editor at *Longreads*. She has a degree in urban planning and writes mainly about cities.

"Recommending a walk from West Hollywood to Hollywood will have locals rolling their eyes and offering a ride but you're a tourist so suck it up; you're not in a hurry"

Ruscha's yard kicking the tyres on his cars (he has a few, including a 1930s Ford truck). But how does this man – who riffed off these oh-so-American motifs of the highway, the motel and the drive-thru – get around? He had just bought an electric car, a Tesla. "Hold on", I thought. "The next thing you know the king of the road will be walking to work."

Recommending a walk from West Hollywood to Hollywood itself will have locals rolling their eyes and offering a ride but you're a tourist so suck it up and relax; you're on two feet and you're not in a hurry. Walking down Sunset is a history lesson: this was the home of counterculture. In 1966 this kind of thing begat Paris in 1968: protest, tough police, long hair, curfews and music. Whisky a Go Go and the place that used to be the Hollywood Hyatt (now an Andaz) were where Stones and Zeppelins crowned themselves in a new Versailles of fresh misdemeanour before Guns N' Roses reinvented the zeal.

On Sunset you're an ant shaded by billboards that are football-fields high and tennis-courts wide and advertise something starring Scarlett Johansson in a catsuit. It's a good job you're walking; if you were in a car you'd crash it. Experienced on foot these hillside-sized invitations to buy an iPhone or see *Star Wars* are *actually* awesome rather than *awesome!* The big bright LA signs of The Golden Spur, the Crown Car Wash, Chili John's and The Body Shop were made to be read and recognised through a windshield at 50 miles per hour but they become intoxicating icebergs of tacky beauty at walking pace. Don't take photographs; why not try thinking an original thought in front of them instead?

As you walk past the Chateau Marmont you'll wonder what all the fuss is about. It looks a bit Scooby Doo but visit the bar at witching hour and you'll see. Past The Body Shop again (they won't fix your bumper but these girls know how to make a dent in your wallet) and you'll descend into Hollywood, where I'll leave you to your own devices. I won't ask questions.

In Los Angeles you're recommended to run, run, run and be slim, Jim but you're considered a crank for taking a walk. Strange, huh? C'mon, cats, we can change all that. All at a strolling pace though please. — (M)

ABOUT THE WRITER: Robert Bound is MONOCLE's
Culture editor and loves Los Angeles for its artists,
sunny disposition and the epic Amoeba Music record
shop. Oh, there's no MONOCLE bureau in LA. Yet.

Culture
—— City of artists

Los Angeles may have risen to fame on the back of the film industry but that's only a small reason why the city is one of the most exciting cultural hubs in the world. The Hollywood set aside, you'll find artists, gallerists, writers, musicians and artisans here in spades.

And while the City of Angels may not have the same art heritage as old-world Europe, it more than makes up for it in the contemporary stakes (plus there's still a surprising amount of classics hanging on its walls). Indeed, not even New York can compete with LA's sheer diversity of museums – from The Getty to The Broad – and there's also a dizzying range of independent cinemas, bookshops and commercial art galleries.

Here's a step-by-step guide to what you can't miss on LA's defiantly diverse culture scene – in between the surf lessons and taco gobbling, of course.

Museums
Artefacts and exhibits

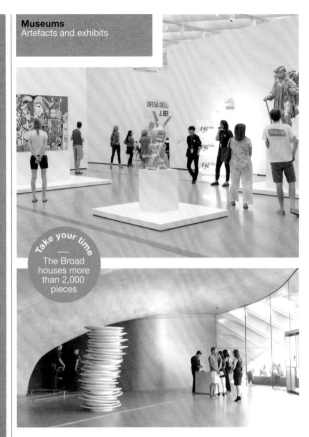

Take your time
——
The Broad houses more than 2,000 pieces

1
The Broad, Downtown
Wide range of art

The vast philanthropic influence of Eli and Edythe Broad is evident throughout LA but nowhere more so than at The Broad, which opened in 2015. "We wanted a museum where we could show art to the public, consolidate our collection in one location and continue loaning artworks to museums around the world," says Eli Broad.

Designed by New York architects Diller Scofidio + Renfro, the three-storey museum features pieces by the likes of Jeff Koons, Cy Twombly, Cindy Sherman, Barbara Kruger, Anselm Kiefer and Ed Ruscha.
221 South Grand Avenue, 90012
+1 213 232 6200
thebroad.org

Good books
———
The library
holds a rare
Gutenberg
Bible

❷

The Huntington, Pasadena
Natural and intellectual delights

Businessman Henry E Huntington
(the chap behind LA's Pacific
Electric Railway, which once
connected the city) established
The Huntington in 1919 in this
mansion, half an hour's drive
from Downtown. The museum
possesses one of the world's
finest research libraries as well
as works by illustrious artists,
meaning you can check out Edward
Hopper's painting "The Long
Leg" before visiting the library
holding the Ellesmere manuscript
of Chaucer's *Canterbury Tales*.

Another major draw is the
garden that blossoms with 15,000
varieties of plants from all corners
of the globe. It is actually made up
of 12 different green spaces; don't
miss the Japanese Garden with
its traditional drum bridge or
the Chinese Garden tea house.
1151 Oxford Road, 91108
+1 626 405 2100
huntington.org

3

Annenberg Space for
Photography, Century City
Captivating developments

The Annenberg Foundation's
Space for Photography gallery is
dedicated to digital imagery and
print photography. The Aecom-
designed venue regularly exhibits
photos and films captured around
the world; past shows include
Refugee, which documented the
plight of 60 million displaced
people through the lenses of Tom
Stoddart, Martin Schoeller, Lynsey
Addario and other photographers of
note. The collection is thoughtfully
curated and there's always
something eye-opening to discover.
2000 Avenue of the Stars, 90067
+1 213 403 3000
annenbergphotospace.org

4

Museum of Contemporary Art
Three of a kind

The Museum of Contemporary Art
(Moca) has three venues showing
post-1940s art: Moca Grand Avenue
displays works by luminaries such
as Jackson Pollock and Mark Rothko,
while the Geffen Contemporary
focuses on experimental art.
The Moca Pacific Design Center
specialises in architecture and design.
Grand Avenue: 250 South Grand
Avenue, 90012
+1 213 626 6222
The Geffen Contemporary: 152 North
Central Avenue, 90012
+1 213 625 4390
Pacific Design Center: 8687 Melrose
Avenue, 90069
+1 310 289 5223
moca.org

*What do you mean you
don't understand? I'm
barking through this
megaphone*

5

Los Angeles County Museum of
Art, Miracle Mile
Comprehensive collection

This institution was founded in
1965 and is today the biggest
art museum in the western US.
The encyclopaedic collection
encompasses about 130,000 objects
from around the globe: everything
from pre-Columbian masterpieces
to contemporary sculptures such as
Michael Heizer's "Levitated Mass".
The museum also incorporates
one of the world's most significant
Islamic art collections and a pavilion
for Japanese art. What's more, its
riches are set to grow even more
once the Peter Zumthor-designed
makeover is completed in 2023.
    Start your visit at Ray's and Stark
Bar: it's a good place to soak up
some Californian sun (and wine)
while mapping out your plan of
attack for this mammoth museum.
5905 Wilshire Boulevard, 90036
+1 323 857 6010
lacma.org

6
Pasadena Museum of California
Art, Pasadena
Envelope-pushing art

At times achingly avant-garde,
PMCA is always likely to provoke
and stimulate. The high-ceilinged,
warehouse-like space has
the unique remit of bringing
Californian design and art to
the people and there's a definite
pop-culture feel to it – just check
out the graffiti in the car park.

Exhibitions change every
three to four months (the nod is
often towards the contemporary
and the abstract), with recent
showings including Brett Weston's
excellent close-up photographs
and Kat Hutter and Roger Lee's
deconstructed view of Cali's
landscape. The museum also
has a sharing agreement with
Crocker Art Museum in
Sacramento, with showcases
tending to travel there after
premiering in LA.
*490 East Union Street, 91101
+1 626 568 3665
pmcaonline.org*

(7)
Hammer Museum, Westwood
Contemporary hits

The Hammer Museum opened
in 1990 and has since partnered
with the neighbouring University
of California. Under director
Ann Philbin it displays about
300 programmes a year; its
contemporary collection numbers
more than 2,000 works by artists
including Catherine Opie, David
Lamelas and Oscar Tuazon.

The museum's offering covers
artist talks, creative workshops
and seminars, while the on-site
Billy Wilder Theater shows an
entire century's worth of moving
pictures, from early silent films to
recent releases. The courtyard of
the Edward Larrabee Barnes-
designed building alone makes
the Hammer Museum worth a look:
scattered with works of art, it's a
square of serenity in the middle
of the city.
*10899 Wilshire Boulevard, 90024
+1 310 443 7000
hammer.ucla.edu*

Sleep on it

The hotel tax you're paying
during your stay helps to
fund LA's cultural institutions,
foremost among them
the Department of Cultural
Affairs, which promotes
arts and creative pursuits
throughout the city.

Four more museums

01 Griffith Observatory,
Los Feliz: Established
in 1935, this art deco
planetarium gives you
the chance to peek
through its Zeiss 12-inch
refracting telescope.
griffithobservatory.org
02 Natural History Museum
Los Angeles County,
Exposition Park: When it
opened in 1913 this beaux
arts venue was one of the
city's first museums.
It documents the region's
history and boasts an
impressive dinosaur exhibit.
nhm.org
03 Petersen Automotive
Museum, Miracle Mile:
This buildling designed
by architecture firm Kohn
Pedersen Fox Associates
showcases more than 300
cars, illustrating the
impact the automobile has
had on life in the US.
petersen.org
04 La Brea Tar Pits and
Museum, Miracle Mile:
The first fossil was
found here in 1875 and
3.5 million fossils later
(including a 6,800kg
Columbian mammoth)
palaeontologists are still
digging in the tar pits of La
Brea. Explore their Ice Age
finds at this museum.
tarpits.org

⑧
Getty Center, Brentwood
Oil paintings and more

Late oil magnate J Paul Getty
began amassing his treasures in the
1930s. Getting to the museum that
today displays them is like escaping
into another world; as you shuttle
up a leafy hilltop in the Santa
Monica Mountains, the cacophony
of cars down on the freeway fades
away just as the sprawling sight of
the city of Los Angeles and its blue
coastline comes into view.

The contemporary construction
of the building itself is a vision
in Italian travertine and was
designed by Richard Meier.
Inside, the art spans statues
from the sixth millennium BC
to contemporary photography
by the likes of Eileen Cowin.

Getty also collected antiques
from the ancient world and these
are on display at the Roman-style
Getty Villa in Pacific Palisades;
it's well worth a visit too.
1200 Getty Center Drive, 90049
+1 310 440 7300
getty.edu

Take it outside

LA is the mural capital of
the world: vibrant street art
by artists such as Cyrcle
and Woodkid, Dabs & Myla
and How & Nosm embellishes
façades across the city and
particularly in Venice, the
Arts District and along
Melrose Avenue.

Commercial galleries
Creative businesses

Sprüth Magers, Miracle Mile
Expansive showcase

Renowned German gallerists
Monika Sprüth and Philomene
Magers founded this light-flooded
two-storey space, set across from
the iconic Lacma (*see page 95*),
in 2016. It's the first US outpost
for the pair. "The idea to open a
branch here arose because we have
so many artists in LA," says director
Anna Helwing.

The expansive wall space and
polished concrete floors provide a
slick backdrop for a solid roster of
exhibitions from the likes of Bernd
& Hilla Becher, Barbara Kruger
and Cindy Sherman, as well as
Peter Fischli & David Weiss and
California's John Baldessari.
Women artists are a particular
focus: "We feature many
idiosyncratic female artists
who have added something
to art history," says Helwing.
5900 Wilshire Boulevard, 90036
+1 323 634 0600
spruethmagers.com

(9)
Norton Simon Museum, Pasadena
Artistic heavyweights

This is simply one of the finest
museums in the US. Housed in
a beautiful modernist building
from 1969 (renovated by Frank
Gehry in 1999), it features
a huge roster of household-
name artists from the old
masters of the Renaissance to the
impressionists, including Raphael,
Cézanne, Renoir, Degas, Van
Gogh, Rembrandt and Picasso.

A blend of the Pasadena Art
Museum's original holdings and
industrialist Norton Simon's own
staggering horde, the collection
stretches to 12,000 pieces although
only 1,000 are on display at any
one time. There is serious breadth
here too, with art spanning from
the 14th century to the present day.
Don't miss the the Asian display
downstairs, the contemporary
Californian offerings or the
tranquil sculpture park.
411 West Colorado Boulevard, 91105
+1 626 449 6840
nortonsimon.org

(2)
Maccarone, Boyle Heights
Creative gathering

More and more New York-based
galleries are setting up in LA (many
just east of the city's Arts District)
but often their branding is so muted
that they are easy to miss. That's
not the case with this 4,600 sq m
complex and its exterior sculpture
garden: Michele Maccarone's LA
outpost, which is twice the size of
her flagship New York gallery, is
impossible to overlook. Accordingly
it has become a meeting place for
the community.

The former warehouse,
converted by Jeff Allsbrook
and Silvia Kuhle of LA-based
architecture and design firm
Standard, showcases Maccarone's
roster of international artists,
comprising Swiss sculptor Carol
Bove, New York-based Nate
Lowman (known for his pop-art-
esque work) and abstract painter
Ryan Sullivan.
300 South Mission Road, 90033
+1 323 406 2587
maccarone.net

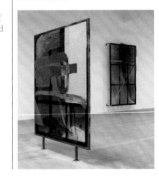

④
M+B, West Hollywood
Room for exploration

Hidden away on a serene street between bustling Melrose Avenue and Santa Monica Boulevard, this petite and unpretentious gallery, founded by Benjamin Trigano, hosts regular exhibitions of North American art with a focus on experimental contemporary photography.

Pieces by Whitney Hubbs, Ellen Carey, Matthew Porter and Nathaniel Mary Quinn have adorned the walls of the one-room space that opened its doors in 2008 in what was once the well-known Asher/Faure Gallery.

"Artists, collectors and writers like to come and hang out here," says director Jonlin Wung. "Our approach is to stay open to everything; there are no rules in art. We like working with artists who push their medium."
612 North Almont Drive, 90069
+1 310 550 0050
mbart.com

③
Hauser Wirth & Schimmel, Arts District
Multidisciplinary appeal

In 2016 Hauser & Wirth, a Swiss gallery founded by Iwan and Manuela Wirth and Ursula Hauser in 1992, transformed what was once a dusty flour mill owned by Globe Mills into the sixth branch of its international gallery network. Creative Space and Selldorf Architects brought new life to the building without erasing its history. Indeed the "GM" monogram is still visible on many of its bannisters and columns.

"Hauser Wirth & Schimmel offers a new model for what a gallery can be today," says Iwan Wirth of the multidisciplinary arts centre. In addition to displaying the work of more than 60 artists, including Maria Lassnig and Hans Arp, the space hosts public talks, book launches, musical performances and craft workshops.
901 East 3rd Street, 90013
+1 213 943 1620
hauserwirthschimmel.com

⑤

Blum & Poe, Culver City
Growing audience

When Timothy Blum and
Jeffrey Poe first opened this
gallery in 1994 they were happy
if they got five visitors a week.
Fast-forward to the present –
two moves and two satellite venues
(in New York and Tokyo) later –
and this international gallery
on the edge of Culver City has
cemented itself as a mainstay of
LA's art scene.

Two spacious floors act as
a blank canvas for rolling
exhibitions that showcase
international artists such as Julian
Hoeber and Julian Schnabel,
as well as Ha Chong-hyun and
Susumu Koshimizu. "The vision
is to continue looking to artists,
old and new, and using the space
for exhibitions, performance
and, very soon, as a bookstore
as well," says Blum.
*2727 South La Cienega
Boulevard, 90034
+1 310 836 2062
blumandpoe.com*

⑥
Gagosian Gallery, Beverly Hills
Taking it to the streets

Local gallery owner Larry Gagosian
opened this flagship in 1995.
Designed by architect Richard
Meier, the clean, geometric space
has a wide glazed aluminium façade
that opens up to the pavement like
a garage door, bringing art to the
car-filled streets of LA. Its two
exhibition halls, including the 2010
expansion characterised by its
unique wood-barrel vault roof, are
diffused with soft light and house
shows by leading contemporary
artists including Anselm Kiefer,
Ed Ruscha, Ellen Gallagher, Cy
Twombly and Jackson Pollock.
*456 North Camden Drive, 90210
+1 310 271 9400
gagosian.com*

Three more galleries

01 **The Box, Arts District:**
Mara McCarthy opened
this venue in 2007 to
showcase artists who
made a name for
themselves in the
1960s and 1970s,
such as Barbara T Smith
and Judith Bernstein.
theboxla.com

02 **The Underground
Museum, Mid-City:**
This gallery was founded
by painter Noah Davis,
who passed away in
2015. The visionary
shows and expressive
installations often touch
upon historic and ongoing
racial divisions.
*theunderground-
museum.org*

03 **Museum as Retail
Space, Boyle Heights:**
What was once a distillery
now encompasses a
bookshop and gallery that
focuses on contemporary
solo shows by the likes
of Elena Stonaker and
Galia Linn.
marsgallery.net

Music venues
Unlimited gigs

①
Echoplex, Echo Park
Close quarters

If it's good enough for The Rolling
Stones (they played here in 2013),
it's good enough for us. Situated just
below its sister venue The Echo, the
Echoplex hosts rock and electronica
performances from the likes of Beck,
Nothing, Skrillex and Wire, plus
reggae and funk nights. It oscillates
between large nightclub and intimate
music venue and can get hot and
sticky – but the atmosphere is
electrifying. If you're in need of a
late-night snack there's cornmeal-
crusted pizzas with Cajun toppings
from Two Boots Pizza, plus taco
trucks, outside.
*1154 Glendale Boulevard, 90026
+1 213 413 8200
theecho.com*

②
Hollywood Bowl, Hollywood
Legendary arena

One of the world's largest natural
amphitheatres, and renowned
summer home of the Los Angeles
Philharmonic, this is undeniably the
city's greatest outdoor music venue.
The Hollywood Bowl first opened
in 1922 and has hosted legends such
as The Beatles and Frank Sinatra.

The white shell framing the stage
was initially designed by Lloyd
Wright (son of Frank) and recently
received a makeover by Hodgetts
+ Fung to bring back the art deco
glamour of the 1920s, which can be
enjoyed from cosy canvas seats and
picnic grounds all year round.
*2301 North Highland Avenue, 90068
+1 323 850 2000
hollywoodbowl.com*

Ⓒ
The Hotel Café, Hollywood
Birthplace of the stars

With its inconspicuous back entrance and refreshing roster of local and international singer-songwriters, this two-stage, acoustically blessed venue is a gem on the northern side of Hollywood's Cahuenga Boulevard, not far from the tacky Walk of Fame. This is the place where The Lumineers and Katy Perry got their starts, where Sara Bareilles made a name for herself and where Adele performed at the outset of her career.

Some nights are busier than others but the nightly line-up, overseen by co-founder Marko Shafer, never disappoints. Three intimate bars in the red-tinged, low-lit club serve well-mixed cocktails, there's ample room to dance (unless it's a packed performance) and everyone's there for the music.
1623 1/2 North Cahuenga Boulevard, 90028
+1 323 461 2040
hotelcafe.com

④
Viper Room, West Hollywood
Scandal magnet

A green neon sign marks the entrance to the club of tabloid headlines on Sunset Boulevard. It opened in 1993 and became a celebrity haunt, thanks in part to its famous former owner Johnny Depp. Prior to that, in the 1950s, it was a jazz club popular with LA gangsters such as Mickey Cohen and Bugsy Siegel.

The venue presents indie and rock shows on the main stage while singer-songwriters belt their hearts out in the lounge downstairs. Right across the road lies another notorious nightspot, Whisky a Go-Go.
8852 Sunset Boulevard, 90069
+1 310 358 1881
viperroom.com

⑤
Amoeba Music, Hollywood
Temple of tunes

First time here? You'll be stunned by the sheer multitude of albums, posters plastered on walls and signs suspended from the ceiling of the world's largest independent record shop (its Hollywood venue takes up a city block). It not only offers cassette tapes, vinyl, CDs and DVDs, it also showcases regular live in-store musical performances. The stage has been graced by the likes of Paul McCartney and Thurston Moore – and while it's dwarfed by the shelves and thousands of records, as soon as the first notes hit everyone is all ears.
6400 Sunset Boulevard, 90028
+1 323 245 6400
amoeba.com

I think a little Bach will really lift the mood in the Viper Room

Film
Silver screens

① New Beverly Cinema, Mid-City
Homage to cinema

The Mediterranean revival-style building that houses this cinema started life as a confectionery company before morphing into a playhouse. Quentin Tarantino saved the family-run cinema from closure in 2010 and is building on its legacy by continuing the tradition of showing back-to-back 35mm or 16mm features.

The single-screen cinema, near CBS Television City, has upgraded its sound system and also installed a 16mm projector to further preserve the classic movie-going experience. Tarantino (and his team) took over programming duties from former owner Michael Torgan; he likes to show films from his personal collection, including rare archival prints such as Henri Verneuil's 1963 thriller *Any Number Can Win* and his own films *Reservoir Dogs* and *Pulp Fiction*.
7165 Beverly Boulevard, 90036
+1 323 938 4038
thenewbev.com

② Cinefamily at the Silent Movie Theatre, Mid-City
Enjoy the silents

Housed in the historic former Silent Movie Theatre dating from 1942, this place remains true to its roots. Every week viewers are given the "silent treatment", which consists of soundtrack-free screenings accompanied by live music.

The cinema puts together an eclectic international programme ranging from contemporary indie films to cult favourites (classics such as Fritz Lang's *Metropolis*). They can all be enjoyed from the cinema's 184-seat auditorium, the walls of which are adorned with monochrome photographs of 20th-century silver-screen stars. Not to be missed are special guest appearances by well-known authors, directors and actors, as well as the parties and pot-luck dinners that take over the space from time to time.
611 North Fairfax Avenue, 90036
+1 323 655 2510
cinefamily.org

Lights, camera, action

The first Hollywood film was made in 1910: D W Griffith's 17-minute 'In Old California'. Many others followed, ushering in Hollywood's Golden Age in the 1930s. The industry remains one of the US's most profitable exports.

LA on film

01 The Big Sleep (1946): Based on author Raymond Chandler's first Philip Marlowe mystery, this film noir starred off-screen couple of the day Humphrey Bogart and Lauren Bacall. An early glimpse into LA's dark side.

02 The Graduate (1967): This ground-breaking film by Mike Nichols, based on the novel by Charles Webb, is a coming-of-age story and a commentary on the Californian lifestyle.

03 Pretty Woman (1990): "This is Hollywood: land of dreams. Some dreams come true, some don't. But keep on dreaming. This is Hollywood." The final words spoken in this modern-day fairy tale reflect the undying appeal of Hollywood.

04 Pulp Fiction (1994): Quentin Tarantino's cult classic – set in LA's backstreets, bars and diners – had a massive impact upon the film industry when it premiered at the Cannes Film Festival in 1994.

05 LA Confidential (1997): Based on James Elroy's masterly crime novel, this is an absorbing, atmospheric portrait of sleazy celebrities and corrupt cops in the LA of the early 1950s.

06 The Big Lebowski (1998): The Coen brothers explore LA's underworld in this comedic indie flick in which a case of mistaken identity turns the life of a loafer into a perilous rollercoaster ride.

07 The Artist (2011): Set in the silent age of 1920s Hollywood, this black-and-white masterpiece tells a tasteful tale of Hollywood fame and fortune.

③
ArcLight Cinema, Hollywood
Commercial free

With its spectacular Cinerama Dome dating back to the 1960s – it's a Los Angeles Historic-Cultural Monument – ArcLight is the ultimate manifestation of a Hollywood cinema. Many of the films lighting up its 15 screens were shot at studios just a short drive away and you never know who you'll spot in the audience.

From headlining blockbusters to limited releases, the range of programming at the cinema complex is as engaging as it is varied. What's more, the US cinema chain doesn't believe in commercials so it's all about film here. The lobby, with its café-cum-bookshop, even doubles as a small museum, exhibiting original costumes and props from recent releases.
6360 Sunset Boulevard, 90028
+1 323 464 1478
arclightcinemas.com

Time for my favourite classic film, 'The Birds'

Drink in the show
—
The Nuart serves beer and wine with its films

④

Nuart Theatre, West Hollywood
Late-night screenings

The Nuart, characterised by its art deco façade and neon signage, first opened on Santa Monica Boulevard in the early 1940s and has made a name for itself by showing a mix of independent and foreign films alongside documentaries and classics. As the flagship of Landmark Cinemas – the nation's largest chain dedicated to independent film – it is a stalwart in the industry.

There's something for everyone, including Saturday night screenings of the longest-running midnight movie *The Rocky Horror Picture Show* (the cinema has a programme of features for so-called "cineinsomniacs"). And as this is Hollywood there's no shortage of events and special appearances from directors and actors such as Miss Sharon Jones, who presented her eponymous documentary here.
11272 Santa Monica Boulevard, 90025
+1 310 473 8530
landmarktheatres.com

Best of the rest
LA media round-up

(1) Print
Reading material

Angelenos are a glossy bunch so it's no surprise there's plenty of handsome lifestyle magazines on offer. Standouts include: lush journal ❶ *Malibu Magazine*, culture mag ❷ *Flaunt* and Jan-Willem Dikkers's arts and fashion title ❸ *Issue*. The best local listings can be found in ❹ *LA Weekly*, a free alternative distributed every Thursday.

The city that fills tabloids the world over also has a few plucky newspapers of its own. The definitive is the Pulitzer Prize-winning ❺ *Los Angeles Times*; the largest metropolitan daily in the US with an average readership of 1.4 million. The city's other big-hitter is Spanish-language ❻ *La Opinión*. Another non-English-language staple is *Korea Daily Los Angeles*.

Kiosks
Shelf life

LA has its fair share of well-stocked print havens, one of which is ❶ *Book Soup* in West Hollywood. Founded by Glenn Goldman in 1975, it stocks 60,000 titles with a special focus on the arts and literary fiction and has a fine selection of global press too. ❷ *Hennessey + Ingalls'* Downtown branch is the place for art, architecture and design books and magazines. If you're looking for a hard-to-find publication your best bet is ❸ *Laurel Canyon News*; open 24/7, this Studio City newsagent stocks hundreds of magazines.

WHERE TO FIND THEM
01 Book Soup
    8818 Sunset Boulevard, 90069
    +1 310 659 3110
02 Hennessey + Ingalls
    300 South Santa Fe Avenue,
    90013
    +1 213 437 2130
03 Laurel Canyon News
    12100 Ventura Boulevard, 91604
    +1 818 769 3327

Radio and podcasts

All those long car journeys along LA's crowded freeways call for good radio shows and podcasts to pass the time. Here's what to tune into:

01 **89.3 KPCC, The Frame:** This daily show broadcast by Pasadena's public radio station is hosted by John Horn and covers Southern California's latest movie, music, TV, arts and entertainment news.
    scpr.org
02 **89.9 KCRW: Which Way, LA?:** Award-winning presenter Warren Olney covers it all in this show, which draws on newsmakers from around the world for its lively discussions.
    kcrw.com
03 **Aloud:** Recorded live at the Los Angeles Public Library, Aloud brings cultural figures together. Past guests have included Ta-Nehisi Coates, Salman Rushdie and Carlos Santana.
    ifla.org
04 **The Conversation:** The homegrown podcast launched in 2011 and features engaging talks between artists, gallerists, collectors, curators, writers and its host, LA artist Michael Shaw.
    theconversationpod.com

The Monocle Daily

It would be remiss not to mention Monocle 24's own radio show that offers a round-up of world news with a focus on the Americas. Our New York bureau and correspondents across the region will ensure that you stay completely up to date.
monocle.com/radio

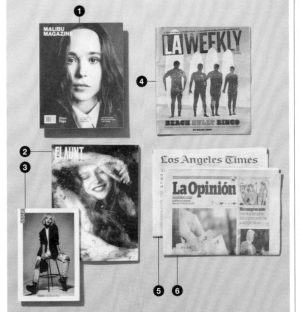

Design and architecture
── City of angles

Once you've got over LA's achingly beautiful topography – from mountains to shore, passing bougainvillea and palms along the way – you'll realise that the built environment is every bit as alluring.

Luminaries such as John Lautner, Frank Lloyd Wright, Richard Neutra and Frank Gehry have all produced some of their finest work here and no trip would be complete without spending a little time in a booth within an iconic Googie-style diner. Then there is the very Southern Californian take on Craftsman houses, centred on pedestrian-friendly Pasadena.

LA hasn't always valued its design heritage as much as it should, but thanks to the rebirth of Downtown, many historic buildings – theatres, office blocks and so on – are in line to receive facelifts in the future. For LA it's another step towards joining the likes of Chicago, New York and Miami as a true American design city.

Postmodern and contemporary
New and exciting

① Cathedral of Our Lady of the Angels, Downtown
Houses of the holy

This cathedral designed by Pritzker Prize-winning Spanish architect José Rafael Moneo is a whopping 11 storeys tall, making it feel more like a compound than a temple of prayer. Construction began in 1999 and was completed in 2002 on a site a few minutes' walk from Walt Disney Concert Hall (*see page 108*). Previously the city's cathedral had been based in the historic Cathedral of Saint Vibiana's (now an events space).

While it has been known to divide opinion, there's little doubt that this space is an impressive feat. The exterior design has been conceived to include almost no right angles, resulting in subtly striking visuals that speak of a city where non-conformity is celebrated. Step inside and you'll see the theme continued in low-hanging triangular-shaped lights, curved wooden benches and the mother of all contemporary organs.
555 West Temple Street, 90012
+1 213 680 5200
olacathedral.org

On the line
—
Trains take 30,000 people per day past the tower

2

Conjunctive Points, Culver City
Exciting developments

Located within the Hayden Tract area of Culver City, Conjunctive Points is a litmus test for how far redevelopment can be pushed. Over the past three decades husband-and-wife developers Frederick and Laurie Samitaur Smith have been buying old warehouses and land and collaborating with architect Eric Owen Moss on some 30 projects. Today, the Tract feels like one of the most buzzing places in LA for avant-garde design.

The most recently completed is Pterodactyl, a jaggedly beautiful office building (*pictured, top left*) that sits atop a parking garage from 1998, nestled between warehouses from the 1940s. Waffle (*pictured, above*) resembles a misshapen cheese grater while the steel-ringed "information" edifice Samitaur Tower (*pictured, right and top right*) incorporates projection screens.
Culver City
ericowenmoss.com

3
Walt Disney Concert Hall,
Downtown
LA's living room

This structure is a shimmering,
disjointed statement from the city's
most famous adopted architect,
Frank Gehry. While unquestionably
impressive inside – watching the
resident LA Philharmonic in the
360-degree concert hall is epic –
the real marvel is the external façade
of steel curves, akin to an LA take
on the Sydney Opera House.

The project began in the late
1980s after a $50m endowment from
Lillian Disney to honour her late
husband. Ten years later the building
still wasn't completed and costs had
blown out to more than $265m.
Happily, private donations rolled in
and the concert hall (which Gehry
described as a "living room for the
city") finally opened in 2003.

Fans should also visit his 1980
Spiller house in Venice and the 1978
Gehry Residence in Santa Monica.
111 South Grand Avenue, 90012
+1 323 850 2000
laphil.com

Modernist
Pioneering places

①

Schindler House, West Hollywood
Inside out

This building by Rudolph Michael Schindler is often cited as the first modernist house in western architecture. The Austrian architect was inspired by Japanese design while working on the Tokyo Imperial Hotel project at Frank Lloyd Wright's office in Wisconsin.

While the materials aren't themselves modernist (wood and plaster are favoured, not glass and steel), the design was certainly something new, focusing on fluid transitions between indoors and out, rather than the established virtue of external beauty.

It was created as four studios for Schindler and his wife and another couple; Richard Neutra (*see page 111*) moved in in the 1920s but soon fell out with Schindler. The property is open Wednesday to Sunday, 11.00 to 18.00; it's now the site for the Mak Center for Art and Architecture.
835 North Kings Road, 90069
+1 323 651 1510
makcenter.org

②
Capitol Records Tower,
West Hollywood
In tune with its surrounds

Drive through West Hollywood to the corner of Hollywood and Vine, not far from the 101, and you'll see this stubby landmark that has hosted the likes of Frank Sinatra and Nat King Cole. And we don't use "landmark" lightly: this 1956 construction from Welton Becket and Associates was the world's first circular office building and, with its spire, the first high-rise to be constructed in West Hollywood after the Second World War. A red light on the top blinks out the letters "H-o-l-l-y-w-o-o-d" in Morse code; at Christmas, it takes on the form of a Christmas tree.
1750 Vine Street, 90028

Three more modernist icons

01 **Stahl House, Hollywood Hills:** Another of the houses from the case-study programme initiated by *Arts and Architecture* magazine *(see page 112)*, Stahl House was designed by Pierre Koenig and finished in 1960. The views from the glass-and-steel modernist icon are incredible. Book a tour in advance.
stahlhouse.com

02 **Sheats Goldstein Residence, Beverly Hills:** With its angular roof and dominant glass, this masterpiece is by one of LA's most famous architects John Lautner, who was heavily influenced by Frank Lloyd Wright. James Goldstein recently donated the house to the Los Angeles County Museum of Art.
jamesfgoldstein.com

03 **Ennis House, Los Feliz:** This home was built by Frank Lloyd Wright's son Lloyd under his father's instructions. It was influenced by temple architecture and made with some 27,000 concrete blocks. Getting a tour is tricky but it's worth a drive by for a glimpse of the façade alone.
ennishouse.com

Downtown dynamo

If you're heading Downtown to Grand Central Market, check out the Bradbury Building opposite. You can't go upstairs but you can marvel from the lobby at this 1893 building with original exposed lift shafts. *304 South Broadway, 90013*

3
Hollyhock House, Los Feliz
Flower power

Frank Lloyd Wright's first LA
home was a clear departure
from his previous "Prairie style"
of architecture. He designed it
for feminist and FBI-scrutinised
communist Aline Barnsdall, who
dreamed of creating a community
for actors on Olive Hill. While her
plans were never fully completed,
the main home was; Barnsdall was
famously unhappy with the results,
however, and never lived there.

Named after her love of hollyhock
flowers, the house is a bold temple-
inspired space, as is evident in
the relief above the fireplace in the
living room. It features a plethora of
modernist traits, from the concept
of contraction and release that's
presented in a narrow entrance
leading to an open hallway, to the
easy transition between the living
room and courtyard. Tours run
Thursday to Sunday, 11.00 to 16.00.
4800 Hollywood Boulevard, 90027
+1 323 913 4031
barnsdall.org

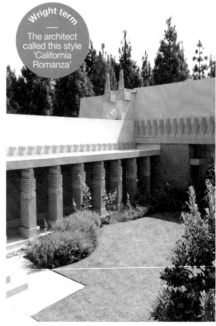

Wright term
——
The architect
called this style
'California
Romanza'

④
Neutra VDL Research House,
Silver Lake
Living in a box

Austrian architect Richard Neutra brought his radical ideas to LA at a time when modernism was little known in the US. This box-like residence – his third in the country and where he lived for almost three decades – was built in 1932 and financed with a small loan and money borrowed from Neutra's friends and family. The building was extremely avant-garde, not just for its use of light and space in a compact area but also for its synthetic materials: among other things it used the kind of steel frames usually employed in skyscrapers.

A 1963 fire destroyed the original home (the 1939 Garden House was the only surviving section) but Richard's son Dion oversaw reconstruction based on the original blueprint.

It's possible to tour the property on Saturdays from 11.00 to 15.00.
2300 Silver Lake Boulevard, 90039
neutra-vdl.org

⑤
Eames House, Pacific Palisades
Time capsule

The Eames House is case study number eight in a series of 25 houses commissioned by John Entenza, editor of *Arts and Architecture* magazine, between the mid-1940s and early 1960s.

A bid to rethink postwar residential living, it was built in the winding hills of the Pacific Palisades as a home for designers Charles and Ray Eames, who moved into it in 1949. The original idea was scrapped because it would have uprooted the site's beautiful eucalyptus trees and the plans were amended to feature two structures (a house and studio), sitting parallel to the meadow and separated by an open courtyard. Making the steel-beamed house viable for the middle class, off-the-shelf products were employed – albeit in unusual ways – including the use of wooden flooring as sidewalls.

The home is still in pristine condition. Its windows and coloured external panels have been preserved by the pair's granddaughter, who has kept the interiors frozen in time. It's open for external visits and fascinating internal guided tours, but make sure to reserve both in advance.
203 Chautauqua Boulevard, 90272
+1 310 459 9663
eamesfoundation.org

Down to earth — Charles called his home 'unself-conscious'

Los Angeles — Design and architecture D

113

Downtown theatres

Nowhere else in the US has such a concentrated collection of historic theatres as Broadway in Downtown. Some are in a state of disrepair, others are being run as shops and one has even been converted into an evangelical church.

01 The Orpheum: This theatre first opened in 1926 as part of LA's vaudeville circuit. It was restored in the late 1980s (the original Mighty Wurlitzer organ was preserved) and still hosts regular music concerts.
laorpheum.com

02 Los Angeles Theatre: You might not get to see the opulent, French baroque-inspired interiors of this 1931 building (the theatre only opens for special events and is often put to use for film shoots) but the sight of the towering neon marquee outside is impressive too.
losangelestheatre.com

03 Tower Theatre: The exterior of this venue is a fantasy blend of baroque revival styles, from Spanish to Moorish, with an old English feel thrown in by the marquee font. It was designed by S Charles Lee – the same architect responsible for the Los Angeles Theatre – and opened in 1927.
towertheatrela.com

Sure you can take a photo of me with my star... I just need to find it...

①
Pasadena City Hall, Pasadena
Hall of fame

Pasadena's city hall is undoubtedly one of the finest in California, if not the US. It was constructed back in 1927 by John Bakewell and Arthur Brown (the duo behind San Francisco's 1915 civic offering) and was influenced by styles such as the early Renaissance, including the work of Andrea Palladio. It's an excellent example of the City Beautiful movement, which gained popularity between the 1890s and the 1920s. A walk through Pasadena will reveal plenty more revivalist gems (*see pages 134 – 135*).
100 North Garfield Avenue, 91101
+1 626 744 4000
ci.pasadena.ca.us

Chapman Plaza, Koreatown
Market leader

The restaurants situated in Chapman Plaza haven't been too considerate with their shop frontages but focus on the details and you'll realise this market is a masterpiece. When it was built in 1927 it was designed for cars; visitors would head into an internal courtyard through a Spanish revival archway.

The façade is concrete worked to resemble sandstone and the space features impressive fortress-like towers in a churrigueresque style (a type of Spanish baroque). Also check out the accompanying Chapman Park Studio building across the road, which is built in a similar fashion.
3451 West 6th Street, 90020

③
The Theatre at Ace
Hotel, Downtown
Inside job

This has to be one of the most
staggering buildings in Los Angeles
– and here it's all about the interiors.
The theatre was constructed in
1927 as a United Artists cinema,
with the backing of silent-film stars
such as Mary Pickford, Douglas
Fairbanks and Charlie Chaplin.
   Its architects, Walker & Eisen,
were inspired by the gothic
architecture of Segovia in Spain
and the detailing they included is
incredible, from the yellow lobby
mirrors installed to make visitors
feel tanned when they arrived in
sunny LA to the mosaic-tiled dome
set within a huge gilded sunburst
ornamentation. And then there are
the extensive murals of studio heads
and matinee idols from yesteryear,
plus the lighting system that throws
up a kaleidoscope of colours, from
yellow to purple.
   The theatre was run as a church
by televangelist Gene Scott in the
1990s (his "Jesus Saves" sign out the
back of the building has been kept
by the Ace team for its ironic value)
before being lovingly restored and
opened in its current guise in 2014;
catch a concert here if you can.
929 South Broadway, 90015
+1 213 235 9614
theatre.acehotel.com

④
San Gabriel Mission
Playhouse, San Gabriel
Custom production

A fine example of the Spanish
revival style, this playhouse was
purpose-built in 1927 by John
Steven McGroarty for a production
of his called *The Mission Play*,
which told the story of LA's
Franciscan forefathers.
   The decadent interiors include
tapestries donated by the King
of Spain, replica chandeliers and
a carved, painted ceiling. And
the façade isn't too shabby either
(although it could do with a fresh
lick of paint): it's a mixture of
Spanish, colonial Mexican and
indigenous styles, based on San
Antonio de Padua in Monterey.
   Be sure to check out the
stunning original mission building
too. One of 21 missions built in
California, it's just a few minutes'
walk away and is a historic
landmark dating back to 1771.
320 South Mission Drive, 91776
+1 626 308 2868
missionplayhouse.org

Googie
Eye-catching ideals

Googling Googie

An offshoot of mid-century modernism, Googie embraced the ideas of progress, technology, travel and the future-forward positivism of the 1940s to 1960s. The aim was to catch the eye with a fusion of impressive curves and jagged edges.

(1)
Union 76 Gas Station,
Beverly Hills
Pump house

Googie is all about sweeping arcs and angles and this petrol station in Beverly Hills is a prime example of both. It was produced by Gin Wong – who would go on to become president of William L Pereira and Associates – and finished in 1965. The design was originally intended for LAX airport as a complement to the Theme Building *(see page 120)* but it ended up moving across town. The station shop isn't anything to write home about but the futuristic roof – with little red squares around the edges and two dominant columns – is striking.
427 North Crescent Drive, 90210
76.com

(2)
Bob's Big Boy, Burbank
Sign of the times

This pioneering building fuses the last days of streamline moderne with a visionary look ahead to the aspirational architecture of the 1950s. Here we see the smooth lines of the former combined with the heavy usage of glass and striking signage of the latter.

The Burbank outlet was constructed in 1949 and designed by Wayne McAllister as the third site in Bob Wian's restaurant empire (the first opened in Glendale in 1936). Today it is the only one of the original buildings left standing although the company itself remains, with franchises in the US and Japan.
4211 West Riverside Drive, 91505

Official status
——
Norm's is a Historic-Cultural Monument

KREISS

470

③

Norm's, West Hollywood
Fine diner

A favourite of senior citizens who like to perch at the bar and order early dinner, this Norm's (open 24 hours) is one of 18 locations from the 1949-established chain.

Although the interiors look a tad tired, the outlet is a time warp – a testament to the 1950s diner. The angular, zigzag sign is a classic and replicated in the shape of the building. This 1957 location was designed by Louis Armet and Eldon Davis and is one of about eight Googie restaurants left in the city.

Ed Ruscha thought it so iconic that he painted it in his 1964 artwork "Norm's, La Cienega, on Fire".
470 La Cienega Boulevard, 90048
normsrestaurants.com

④
Chips, Hawthorne
Jag yourself a coffee

Chips, located in a neighbourhood
southeast of the international
airport, is another fine example of
a Googie coffee shop. Designed
in 1957 by Harry Harrison – the
architect behind Ritts Furniture
shop in West Hollywood – the
building, like Norm's *(see page 117)*,
has been in continuous use since
its inception. The interiors are
pretty much untouched but it's
the jutting, jagged sign that again
threatens to steal the show. The
zigzag theme continues on the roof
of the building – a visual lure for
those all-important customers as
they drive by.
*11908 Hawthorne Boulevard, 90250
+1 310 679 2947*

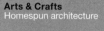
Arts & Crafts
Homespun architecture

❶
Gamble House, Pasadena
Not-so-little prairie house

The idea of prairie architecture was
to be functional while elevating the
home to an artform. Nowhere is this
realised in such epic proportions as
in Pasadena's 1908 Gamble House.
Built by Cincinnati architecture
firm Greene & Greene for David
and Mary Gamble (of the Procter
& Gamble dynasty), its façade
is noteworthy for its redwood
shakes (mostly original) and vast
overhanging wooden eaves that
show a Japanese influence.
    Inside is dedicated to detail and
aesthetics. Wood dominates – from
mahogany to Burmese teak – and
can be seen in both finger-lap and
scarf joints (the latter inspired by
shipbuilding). The quarter-sawn
white-oak flooring in the hall, living
room and dining room has been
laid diagonally to make sure
the carpets don't look crooked.
A tour is highly recommended.
*4 Westmoreland Place, 91103
+1 626 793 3334
gamblehouse.org*

②
Bungalow Heaven, Pasadena
Historic 'hood

Head to an area in Pasadena
bordered by the main thoroughfares
of Orange Grove and Washington,
and the quieter Lake and Hill
streets, and you'll find yourself in
a calm, leafy neighbourhood with
a remarkable number of Arts and
Crafts-style homes. Indeed, within
its 16-block radius (with the best
examples concentrated on just a
few streets) you'll stumble across
more than 800 of these bungalows,
most of them built between 1900
and the 1930s, still in excellent
condition and tended by proud
residents. There are also some
300 residences from the revivals
period of the 1920s. The
neighbourhood (referred to now
as Bungalow Heaven) was granted
landmark status in 1989.

    The land where the houses
were built was originally annexed
by the city in 1909; previously it
had been farmland. Pasadena's
population quadrupled in the
first two decades of the 20th
century and, with the bungalow
well suited to Southern California's
climate. it became an affordable
middle-class option (a new home
cost about $2,500).

    Wandering the streets is like
being transported back in time.
One standout is 1175 Mar Vista
Avenue: designed by architect
Norman F Marsh, this home
was built for George and Fannie
Cram in 1912. It is probably the
most detailed of the houses, with
impressive eaves, barn shakes
and a stacked-timber effect for
the roof.

    Another good example of an
"airplane-style" bungalow (the
name came into use in around
1911 and was taken from the
so-called "airplane rooms" on
the upper storey) can be found
at 734 Holliston. Then there's
1085 North Michigan Avenue,
a "Japanese-Swiss" bungalow
designed and built by Kieft &
Hetherington in 1911. The
low-gabled roof is supported
by double beams resting on
double wood columns and flared
stucco pedestals.
bungalowheaven.org

①
Theme Building, Westchester
The shape of things to come

Completed in 1961, the Theme Building at LAX was intended to signal the exploration of the age and the importance of LA's international airport, which had undergone an expansion. A spaceship-inspired construction with almost animalistic legs, it housed a restaurant (which closed in 2013) but over the years has often been mistaken for the airport's control tower. Another example of Googie architecture (*see page 116*), it cost $2.2m at the time and was overseen by Gin Wong, chief designer at Pereira & Luckman. The observation deck opens some weekends.
209 World Way, 90045
lawa.org

I never fly without my monocle. And a copy of Monocle, of course

②
LA Union Station, Downtown
Expert training

Ok, so it's in a slightly gritty part of Downtown but this is undeniably one of North America's great transport hubs. Dating from 1939, it is recognised as the last grand railroad station built in the US (New York's Grand Central, for example, was constructed much earlier in 1913). Designed by father-and-son team John and Donald Parkinson, it's a blend of art deco and Spanish colonial revival although the roof gable feels a little Arts and Crafts from inside. Los Angeles Conservancy organises Saturday walking tours of the building.
800 North Alameda Street, 90012
+1 213 452 0200
metrolinktrains.com

Big smoke
———
The station is western US's largest train terminal

①
Hollywood sign
Spelling it out

Arguably nothing has promoted LA's brand quite like the iconic, white-lettered sign in the hills of Griffith Park. Erected in 1923 with the help of mules and tractors, it was an advert for a housing development – the city's main source of income at the time – called "Hollywoodland". Intended to be temporary, the sign was an instant hit, achieving notoriety in 1932 when a young actress jumped from one of the letters to her death. In 1949 the sign was refurbished and the "land" removed from the end; this original sign was later demolished and replaced in 1978 with the current version. Hike to Griffith Park, via the observatory, for the best views.

②
LA river
Go with the flow

Floods used to be a constant problem in and around Los Angeles. Waters washed away the original LA *pueblo* (village) in 1815 and when flooding caused $10m worth of damages just under a century later action was taken. A lengthy and painful process of creating concrete channels along the river to prevent flooding began but when taxpayers wouldn't stump up the funds army engineers stepped in, paving the riverbed with concrete between 1938 and 1960. Both bizarre and iconic, it gained star status in the famous car-racing scene from *Grease*.

③
Programmatic architecture
What you see is what you get

Sadly this is an artform that has all but died in LA but there are still examples if you look hard enough.

Like Googie, designs were aimed at catching the eye of motorists zooming past. Programmatic architecture used a thematic approach, making buildings look like items of food or even animals. A fine example is The Idle Hour bar, shaped like a beer barrel and refurbished in 2015. Also check out the giant doughnut at Randy's Donuts near the airport and The Darkroom at 5364 Wilshire Boulevard – the camera shop is gone but the frontage, shaped like a giant Argus camera, remains.

④
Spaghetti junctions
Drive time

The car dominates LA and, despite the frantic experience of driving in the city, there's an odd beauty to the endless signs announcing "smog tests" and the curving mishmash of motorway lanes snaking around each other. Most famous of them all is the Four Level Interchange – sometimes referred to as "The Stack". A world first when constructed 1949, it has lanes shooting off from it in every direction traffic might take. The structure actually wasn't put into use until 1953 as it had to wait for the connecting freeways it was serving to be completed. The looping cloverleaf model has since been reproduced in other US cities and around the world.
958 Boston Street, 90012

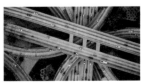

Sport and fitness
—— Healthy interests

Thanks to its sunny disposition, varied topography and idyllic geographical location next to the Pacific Ocean, LA offers a breadth of outdoor activities and athletic thrills. The City of Angels is blessed with formidable hiking trails, steady surfing waves and endless sandy beaches.

As you would expect from the home of Hollywood, most people are preoccupied with looking good (and being well-groomed), so think of a fitness craze and there's a good chance it first took off here. Surfing may have been born in Hawaii but it didn't gain momentum until surfboards made an appearance in LA. The world's first beach volleyball tournament was held here in 1924 and who hasn't heard of Muscle Beach?

Throughout this section we lay out the best ways to make the most of the city's coastline, nature trails and pools to stay in shape during your visit. And don't worry, we list plenty of options for those rare days when the sun isn't shining.

Seaside activities
Shore things

Surf's up
—
Malibu is home to a number of breaks

❶
Surfing, Surfrider Beach
Board meetings

In the latter half of the 19th century three Hawaiian princes introduced surfing to California; they would ride the waves along Santa Cruz on boards handcrafted from local redwood. The trend caught on and led to the first Pacific Coast Surfriding Championships in 1928, but it was in the 1950s when surfing really took off in LA, helped along by the release of surfer-themed songs and films such as *Gidget*. Between 1956 and 1962 the number of California surfers rocketed from 5,000 to more than 100,000. Surfing is still an essential part of the Southern Californian lifestyle today.

One of the best surfing beaches is Malibu Lagoon State Beach, also known as Surfrider Beach; you can pick up a board from the Malibu Surf Shack down the road.
23050 Pacific Coast Highway, Malibu, 90265
malibusurfshack.com

Sailing, Marina del Rey
Ahoy there

Marina del Rey is the largest manmade marina in the US and LA's top destination for sailing and water sports. Pick your vessel at one of the myriad boat-charter services (try Marina del Rey Boat Rentals, which leases everything from kayaks to sloops) or learn the sailing ropes at the California Sailing Academy.
Marina del Rey, 90292
visitmarinadelrey.com

Mat matters
—
With their love of laidback, healthy living, Angelenos are unsurprisingly big yoga enthusiasts. Good yoga studios are as plentiful here as convenience stores, but we suggest you try the daily outdoor sessions on Runyon Canyon. Just bring a mat and a donation.

3

Beach Volleyball, Santa Monica
Set for action

Legend has it that the world's first volleyball nets were pitched here in the 1920s. Today there are courts north and south of Santa Monica Pier. These are very popular, especially on the weekends; courts are generally first-come, first-served but can be reserved for big games.
1550 Pacific Coast Highway, 90401 smgov.net

4

Roller-skating, Venice
Blade runners

Although roller-skating was dreamed up in 1760s London by Belgian John Merlin, Venice Beach became the heartland of the pastime. Indeed in 1979 the mayor of Los Angeles declared Venice Beach "the skating capital of the world". It was in that decade especially that its paved boardwalks teemed with girls on four-wheeled skates, earning themselves the nickname the "Venice Beach Roller Babes".

While the skates have long been replaced by rollerblades, this retro sport is still popular, particularly along The Strand (the weekend roller disco is a highlight). You can rent wheels at numerous shops along Ocean Front Walk.

Spectator sports

As befits LA's status as the US entertainment capital, the city's big sporting events are always superbly orchestrated and enjoyable public spectacles.

01   Baseball
The city's Department of Parks and Recreation offers 110 fields for amateur baseball but to see some top-quality games, visit Dodger Stadium, home to the city's premier team, the Los Angeles Dodgers. The season usually runs from April to September.
losangeles.dodgers.mlb.com

02   Basketball
You're never far from an informal game of basketball on one of the many public-access courts. To watch some top-class playing however (and possibly some celebrity spectators), catch the LA Lakers in Downtown's Staple Center from October to April.
nba.com/lakers

03   Football
LA was without an NFL team for more than 20 years until the return of the Rams from Missouri in 2016. Home games are played at the Memorial Coliseum from September to January.
therams.com

5

Skateboarding, citywide
Hit the deck

Skateboarding was invented in the 1950s when surfing was all the craze; it was something to do when the waves weren't breaking and was referred to as "sidewalk surfing" (singers Brian Wilson and Roger Christian dedicated a song to it). The first boards were homemade: companies such as Makaha and Hobie started production in the 1960s. The first skate contest was held on Hermosa Beach in 1963.

Skating hotspots include the steps at Hollywood High, the West LA Courthouse and the ledges surrounding the Staples Center. But the best place to watch is the park at Venice Beach; just keep an eye out for flying boards.

Top three indoor gyms

01 **The Gym on Nemo, West Hollywood:** Fedele De Santis opened this gym in 1997 to offer a private training facility that feels as if you're working out in your own home (albeit one with state-of-the-art exercise equipment). You can book a session with an in-house trainer or bring along your own if you prefer.
gymonnemo.com

02 **Sandbox Fitness, West Hollywood:** David and Minna Herskowitz were inspired to bring the beach indoors and create this unique exercise space in 2014 after noticing the benefits of training on sand. The full-body workout classes in the 56 sq m sandbox (many of which utilise surfboards) will bring a holiday vibe to your workout.
sandbox-fitness.com

03 **Set and Flow Yoga, West Hollywood:** This yoga studio, founded by Seth Manheimer in 2016, offers nearly 150 classes a week such as yoga, bootcamp, pilates and barre exercises for ultimate results.
setandflowyoga.com

The Santa Monica Stairs

These two staircases near Pacific Palisades have a total of 369 steps, making them a popular training course. Be like the Angelenos and mix your climbing routine up with sets of jumps, sit-ups, push-ups and stretches.

---

⑥
Muscle Beach, Santa Monica
Get pumped

When the Muscle Beach outdoor gym opened south of the pier in 1933, it was quickly colonised by gymnasts, acrobats, stuntmen, wrestlers, weightlifters and circus performers and became the world's most famous work-out spot. By 1951 a second location, the Venice Beach "Weight Pen" (known as Muscle Beach Venice) was added.

No visit to LA would be complete without at least a gander at the heavily muscled folk that frequent this gym – if you're not shy you can join them for a workout (a day pass costs $10/€9).
Ocean Front Walk, Santa Monica, 90401

❶
Culver City Plunge, Culver City
Lap of luxury

Opened in 1949, this 3,700 sq m aquatic venue comprises a heated 50-metre Olympic-size pool plus one and three-metre springboards. Lounge in the sun and enjoy the striking backdrop of the towering Veterans Memorial Building.
4175 Overland Avenue, 90230
+1 310 253 6680
culvercity.org

②
Annenberg Community Beach House Pool, Santa Monica
Ocean views

This marble pool originally belonged to the Marion Davies Estate; it was built for the actress by publishing magnate William Randolph Hearst in the 1920s. Right on the beach, it has views of the ocean and once hosted the likes of Charlie Chaplin and Greta Garbo. Decades later it landed with the State of California and was made available to the public in 2009 as the Annenberg Community Beach House. The pool is open from June to September.
415 Pacific Coast Highway, 90402
+1 310 458 4904
annenbergbeachhouse.com

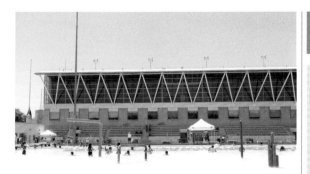

③

John C Argue Swim Stadium,
Exposition Park
Gold-medal facility

Gliding through the pool at the
Los Angeles Olympics Swim
Stadium, as it was once called,
gives you a hint of what it must
feel like to be an Olympian. Built
for the 1932 Summer Games,
this pool of champions in LA's
Exposition Park has seen more
than 65 world records set in
its lanes. US swimmers Buster
Crabbe and Eleanor Holm (both
of whom later found stardom on
the silver screen) were two of the
many champs who received gold
medals in the art deco stadium.

Operated by the LA City
Department of Recreation
and Parks, the year-round
facility reopened in 2004 after
extensive renovations. It features
a 50-metre competition lap pool,
a recreation pool and the Expo
Center sports complex.
3980 Bill Robertson Lane, 90037
+1 213 763 0129
laparks.org

*I better learn how to
skate if I'm going
to hang out in
'Dogtown'*

Hair care and pampering

01 Baxter Finley Barber &
Shop, West Hollywood:
Baxter Finley relocated to
LA from New York in the
1960s. Five years later he
established Baxter of
California and launched
Super Shape, a men's
moisturiser that quickly
achieved cult status. The
brand's first retail space
and barbershop opened in
2010; here you can
purchase the entire range
of products and get your
hair expertly cut (and
your beard trimmed) in
antique barber chairs.
baxterfinley.com

02 Mêche Salon, Beverly
Hills: Tracey Cunningham
and Neil Weisberg
founded Beverly Hills hair
and beauty salon Mêche
(French for 'highlights';
Cunningham is LA's number
one colourist) in 2012. The
contemporary space on
Burton Way was designed
by Rodney Ross and
features marble and
reclaimed-walnut
furnishings. Its library of
magazines to make the
time fly is also impressive.
mechesalonla.com

03 Blind Barber, Culver City:
Enjoy a drink post-trim?
Head to Jeff Laub, Adam
Kirsch and Josh Boyd's
Blind Barber. If you
didn't know better, you
would never guess this
unpretentious barbers on
Washington Boulevard
had a speakeasy-style
bar in the back. We
recommend the Sweeney
Ted, a whisky cocktail
aptly named after the
infamous demon barber.
blindbarber.com

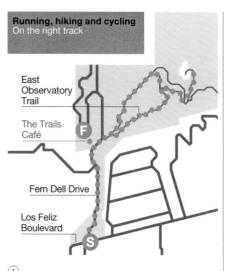

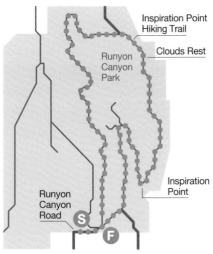

①

Griffith Park to Observatory run
Watch where you're running

DISTANCE: 7km
GRADIENT: Hilly
DIFFICULTY: Advanced
HIGHLIGHT: Views over LA from Griffith Observatory
BEST TIME: During the day on weekends (after 12.00), when the observatory and The Trails Café are open

Established in 1935, Griffith Observatory was one of the first planetariums in the US. At 350 metres above sea level it offers unparalleled views of the city, including the Hollywood Sign. This run across Mount Hollywood and up to the observatory is challenging but rewarding.

Enter Griffith Park at Fern Dell Drive off Los Feliz Boulevard and follow the path upwards into the hills. The leisurely track through rainforest-like surroundings soon turns into a strenuous run over arid mountain ground.

When you pass The Trails Café on your left, take the next right onto the East Observatory Trail. At the next intersection you come to, turn right. Snake your way uphill to the observatory (you'll see the dome up ahead), keeping an eye out for the Hollywood Sign and being alert to any horses that may be using the path too.

When you reach the lookout, either take a break and enjoy the panoramic views or do some elevated lunges and skip-ups on the wooden benches.

This final stretch up to the summit is the steepest part of the trail. Once you've reached the observatory, climb up to the roof and check out the telescope dome. Then return on the track back to the lookout and make a right once you reach a fork in the road to join the Firebreak Trail. Continue all the way down to Fern Dell Drive and finish your run with refreshments at The Trails Café (open from 08.00 to 17.00); the pies and sandwiches are never disappointing.

②

Runyon Canyon run
Urban wilderness

DISTANCE: 2.7km
GRADIENT: Hilly
DIFFICULTY: Moderate
HIGHLIGHT: Views of Hollywood and beyond
BEST TIME: Sunset

Runyon Canyon is a 55-hectare park in the centre of Hollywood with excellent views (in winter or spring you'll be able to see all the way to the Pacific Ocean). It was acquired by the City of Los Angeles in 1983 and is managed by the Department of Recreation and Parks as an "urban wilderness". It's easily accessed from North Vista Street in Hollywood Hills.

Warm up with a jog up Runyon Canyon Road; you'll see the gates for the park up ahead. Enter and veer left for the clockwise route, which offers a more gradual ascent.

Follow the path all the way around, keeping right at the intersections, and continue down Inspiration Point Hiking Trail. You'll soon reach the Clouds Rest viewpoint, which overlooks the city at 314 metres. Take a seat on the bench to have a breather and enjoy the vista for a moment or two.

When you're ready, follow the path as it meanders down to Inspiration Point, another striking vantage point offering views out over Hollywood. From here continue on the path leading downhill, bearing left at the major intersection to stay on the main track. When you reach a set of gates, pass through and continue on.

After a short time you'll make your way past a line of palm trees and reach a clearing. Look to your right and you'll see a path leading slightly uphill, which will take you back to the starting point on Runyon Canyon Road.

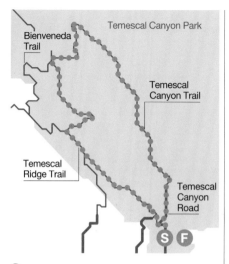

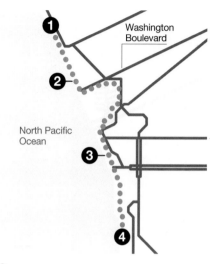

③
Temescal Gateway Park hike
Loop trail

DISTANCE: 4.8km
GRADIENT: Hilly
DIFFICULTY: Moderate
HIGHLIGHT: Views of Santa Barbara and the Pacific coast
BEST TIME: Mornings (before work) or weekends

Temescal Canyon Trail is a picturesque 4km loop trail in the Pacific Palisades. Be sure to wear appropriate footwear and keep an eye out for rattlesnakes.

Enter the Temescal Gateway Park, pass by the camping shop and you'll see a signpost on the far side of the car park. Take the path to the left that leads to the Temescal Ridge Trail. You will soon see a set of stairs next to the hike's mileage sign; the path is narrow and steep so take care. Ascend through the thicket of the Ridge Trail, veering right at all intersections you pass. Don't forget to take in the breathtaking views over LA's coastline as you ascend.

When you've passed the Bienveneda Trail junction you will reach the intersection of Temescal Canyon Trail. Turn right to stay on the loop (another option is to delve deeper into the Santa Monica Mountains and visit Skull Rock).

You'll pass from desert-like terrain into a leafy forest surrounded by oaks and sycamores. Continue until you reach a wooden footbridge. Here (if there's been sufficient rainfall) you can watch the stream flow from a bubbling waterfall.

After another 800 metres of gradual descent the trail becomes a woodland walk, followed by a luscious green park. This is a good place to stop for a picnic if you've brought supplies. To finish, carry on down the path until you reach a collection of wooden cabins and then familiar territory: the car park.

④
Marvin Braude 'The Strand' cycle
Coastal pedal

DISTANCE: 35km (70km return trip)
GRADIENT: Flat
DIFFICULTY: Easy
HIGHLIGHT: Hermosa Beach, Marina del Rey and Santa Monica Beach
BEST TIME: Sunny mornings or afternoons

The Marvin Braude Bicycle Path is a 35km trail from Pacific Palisades to the City of Torrance. The majority of the route follows a wide concrete path shared with pedestrians, runners and skaters, so take it easy and enjoy the beautiful beach views.

Jump on your beach cruiser at ❶ *Will Rogers State Beach* and head towards Santa Monica. After passing the pier continue through Venice Beach. You'll recognise the lively promenade from Hollywood movies; be sure to check out ❷ *Muscle Beach* as you pass.

When you reach the main thoroughfare, Washington Boulevard, turn left (a slight detour is required to circle around Marina del Rey). Continue for 800 metres or so until you see Marvin Braude Bike Path leading to the right (it's just after the small body of water you'll pass on your right-hand side). Follow this trail; it will cross over Admiralty Way, lead through a car park and then veer right when it hits Ballona Creek. You will eventually cross the creek and rejoin the beachside cycling route.

As you near Dockweiler State Beach you'll be close enough to LAX Airport to count the planes taking off. Cycle on through El Segundo until you reach the beautiful community of ❸ *Manhattan Beach* (if the swell is suitable you can stop for a surf).

Continue on past Hermosa Beach. When you reach ❹ *Redondo Beach*, you'll see a snack shop, a perfect spot to refuel before hitting the road for the return trip.

Walks
—— Leave the car behind

There's no denying that Los Angeles is a city that relies on cars and that you're generally hard-pressed to get around without one. But there are still neighbourhoods where walkers can take their time exploring, areas filled with cafés, galleries, restaurants and picturesque views – places that are about more than simply passing through. Here's our guide to making tracks in LA without leaving a huge carbon footprint.

NEIGHBOURHOOD 01
Silver Lake
All that glitters

Silver Lake's name has nothing to do with the colour of its reservoir but this neighbourhood 8km northwest of Downtown did go by a different name before the artificial lake was created. Scotsman Hugo Reid christened it Ivanhoe in the late 1800s (referring to the Scottish novel of the same name) because the area's rolling hills reminded him of his homeland. Today many of the streets here still carry Scottish names and you can climb said hills via a number of brightly painted outdoor staircases.

More than a century later, Silver Lake has seen an influx of young creative people populating the hills and opening small businesses. The pole of influence – once centred on Venice – has very much shifted eastwards to places such as this, alongside nearby Echo Park and up-and-coming Highland Park. All the Silver Lake chatter has merit: this rare walkable neighbourhood has a hefty array of choice retail, bars and restaurants, all of which are well documented in this guide. You'll find countless cosy neighbourhood restaurants, well-stocked boutiques, cocktail bars and coffee shops, as well as food trucks and farmer's markets.

If you want a barometer of what's happening in LA, Silver Lake is not a bad place to start.

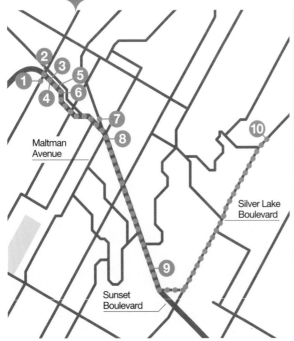

Maltman Avenue

Silver Lake Boulevard

Sunset Boulevard

Road to riches
Silver Lake walk

With any walk you may want to start with some fuel. You could stand in the lengthy queue at Intelligentsia Coffee but there's more joy in taking a table next door in ❶ *Café Stella's* enclosed garden, sipping a flat white and reading the paper or checking out the area's pretty young things.

Around the corner is the ❷ *Cheese Store of Silver Lake*. This tiny shop packs in wine and pantry

Address book

01 Café Stella
3932 Sunset Boulevard
+1 323 666 0265
cafestella.com

02 Cheese Store of
Silver Lake
3926 Sunset Boulevard
+1 323 644 7511
cheesestoreofsilverlake.com

03 Clementine Floral Works
3936 Sunset Boulevard
+1 323 662 2808
clementinefloralworks.com

04 Bar Keeper
3910 Sunset Boulevard
+1 323 669 1675
barkeepersilverlake.com

05 Juice Served Here
3827 Sunset Boulevard
+1 323 522 6260
juiceservedhere.com

06 Spice Station
3819 Sunset Boulevard
+1 323 660 2565
spicestationsilverlake.com

07 Pine & Crane
1521 Griffith Park
Boulevard
+1 323 668 1128
pineandcrane.com

08 Buck Mason
3532 Sunset Boulevard
+1 323 522 3156
buckmason.com

09 The Thirsty Crow
2939 Sunset Boulevard
+1 323 661 6007
thirstycrowbar.com

10 The Satellite
1717 Silver Lake
Boulevard
+1 323 661 4380
thesatellitela.com

staples as well as cured meats and olives; the friendly staff will let you taste-test a few. It's likely that the adjacent shop has caught your attention too: ❸ *Clementine Floral Works* is packed with a rainbow of flowers, with bouquets wrapped in newspaper. You'll also find petite hanging planters and small (read: packable) vases.

Head back to the pavement and take a right. A few metres down is ❹ *Bar Keeper*, where you can find bitters, small-batch spirits and some incredible vintage barware. The spirits and glassware inventory changes regularly so a visit will always be a pleasure – and often inspiring if you like to tend a bar at home. Continue to the corner at Hyperion Avenue and dart across the street to ❺ *Juice Served Here*. There's plenty of cold-pressed goodness to keep your energy up and the beautiful glass bottles are handy if you're keen on keeping fluids with you on your trek.

A few doors down, hidden along a tree-lined alley, is ❻ *Spice Station*. This hole-in-the-wall shop packs in about 400 spices, herbs, salts, sugars, peppercorns and chillies, all displayed in glass jars.

Continue on the same route, passing Lucile Avenue and Edgecliff Drive, until you reach a small grassy area on your left. Cross it to Griffith Park Boulevard where you'll find ❼ *Pine & Crane*. This casual lunch and dinner spot serves Chinese and Thai plates in modern surrounds. The menu is small but the beef noodle soup and traditional Taiwanese *sanbeiji* ("three-cup chicken") are excellent.

There's plenty of shopping to be done in Silver Lake (*see pages 48 – 68*) but continue back on the other side of Sunset to ❽ *Buck Mason*. This LA brand sells simple "made in America" T-shirts and denim worth stocking up on.

Eventually cross to the other side of Sunset Boulevard and continue in the same direction. It will likely be cocktail hour by now; it's a 10-minute walk to ❾ *The Thirsty Crow*. This is a whiskey bar but the menu has a little something for everyone: a mezcal and ginger-rhubarb-strawberry number, tequila tipples or a classic old fashioned, for example.

If you still have some energy, continue walking until you reach Silver Lake Boulevard and turn left. A journey of about 12 minutes will take you to ❿ *The Satellite*, where indie rock bands have been putting on shows since it was Spaceland in the mid-1990s. There's something happening every night of the week here – including Dance Yourself Clean every Saturday (a lights and music DJ set) – so check the calendar.

Getting there

The most convenient way to visit Silver Lake is by car: for parking there's often metered space on Sunset or you could look for a two-hour spot on Hyperion Avenue. If you don't have your own chariot, bus 704 serves both Hyperion Avenue and Sunset from Downtown.

NEIGHBOURHOOD 02
Los Feliz
Casual community

Bordered by Little Armenia to the west and Silver Lake to the east, Los Feliz is a tranquil nugget of Hollywood that has managed to maintain a strong sense of identity – and a decidedly laidback one at that. Hemmed by Griffith Park (a constant reminder of the natural beauty of the area), Los Feliz is dominated by two main thoroughfares – Hillhurst Avenue and North Vermont Avenue – that can cater to all your possible vices, from caffeine and booze to food and small boutiques.

The roots of Los Feliz can be traced back to LA's early days: José Vicente Feliz had been appointed commissioner of the Pueblo of Los Angeles in 1787, the early Spanish settlement village founded six years earlier that would spend time as part of Mexico and eventually morph into the US metropolis it is today. In exchange for his services Feliz was granted a ranch in the neighbourhood that would take his family name. Today, there are still remnants of that past in the form of a Rancho Los Feliz adobe house in Griffith Park dating from the 1830s.

In a city relentlessly driving forward (both figuratively and literally) Los Feliz feels like a slower, less frenetic antidote. And if you're able to time a trip to tie in with the flowering purple jacarandas lining the neighbourhood's boulevards you'll leave with an extra spring in your step.

Find your happy place
Los Feliz walk

With the park and Griffith Observatory behind you, walk south on Hillhurst Avenue (from Los Feliz Boulevard) until you reach ❶ *Little Dom's* on the corner of the aptly named Avocado Street. This favourite is an excellent pit stop for eggs or lunch and there is outdoor seating; check out the wooden bar and stained-glass windows and take your time perusing the newspaper that comes on a wooden reading stick.

Once you're done continue south past the neon sign of Hillhurst Liquor (nope, it's too early for that) and then cross over and turn right at Finely Avenue. On your left is ❷ *St Mary of the Angels Church*, built in 1930 and funded by silent-movie star Mary Pickford, among others. Designed by Carlton Winslow Senior, it's a fascinating mishmash of styles, from the Spanish colonial revival exterior to the gothic arches inside (be sure to check out the Italian altarpiece from 1475).

Head back to Hillhurst Avenue and turn right. On the next corner is ❸ *Carol Young Undesigned*, a women's clothing boutique that has been in the area for a decade and where all the clothing is made on-site using fabrics such as cotton and hemp. There are also accessories, jewellery and shoes from other brands. Next door is ❹ *Vamp*, another women's shop, this time focused on shoes; it's a reliable stockist for LA designers such as Remix and Charlotte Stone. It's also worth a quick dash across the road to record shop

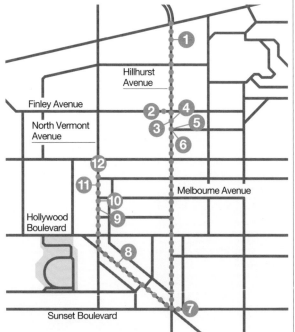

Ⓢ *High-Fidelity*, which sells mostly secondhand vinyl but is also a decent place to pick up flyers for gigs. Next door you'll see the excellent Ⓢ *Jeni's* ice cream shop and although you haven't walked far yet it's probably time for a reward: a Riesling poached-pear sorbet or the salty caramel will do.

South of this point the outlets become a little more mixed: you'll pass Celebrity Cleaners (this is Hollywood) and then the public library. It gets a little downmarket but push through to Hollywood Boulevard and then loop round to the left onto Sunset Boulevard. You can't miss the garish red paint of Ⓢ *Vista Theater*, a decidedly eccentric cinema from 1923 that plays both old and new pictures.

Retrace your steps onto Hollywood Boulevard and head northwest towards North Vermont Avenue. On the way you'll pass the excellent Hotel Covell (*see page 23*), which has an excellent bar (*see page 47*). Next up is the bizarre offering that is Ⓢ *Soap Plant & Wacko*, a tasteless and tacky but undeniably amusing shop-cum-gallery that sells everything from mystical books to African barber's shop signs.

Sanity returns as you veer right onto North Vermont Avenue. On the left-hand side of the road you'll come to classic Hollywood dive-chic restaurant Ⓢ *The Dresden*. It's worth sticking in the area to sip a cocktail and check out a show from Marty and Elayne, an old-time crooning couple who have been playing at the venue for 35 years. A little further up on the same side is ⑩ *Belljar*, a womenswear shop that has some Californian present options such as PF Candle Co and La Tierra Sagrada cosmetics.

Heading northwards you'll immediately hit ⑪ *The Arts Annex*, sister of the larger original bookshop Skylight Books next door. The venue has a great selection of art, design and music books, as well as graphic novels and a newsstand of mags. Your final stop is for a much-needed caffeine hit at ⑫ *Bru Coffeebar* just before Franklin. Rest those legs and check out the contemporary art over a brew. Or do we mean bru?

Getting there

The Metro Rapid 780 bus runs from either Hollywood or Glendale and stops on Los Feliz Boulevard. If you are travelling by tram, the closest station to the area is Vermont/ Sunset on the Red Line, which snakes its way from Union Station in Downtown to North Hollywood.

Address book

01 Little Dom's
    2128 Hillhurst Avenue
    +1 323 661 0055
    littledoms.com

02 St Mary of the Angels Church
    4510 Finley Avenue
    +1 323 660 2700

03 Carol Young Undesigned
    1953 1/2 Hillhurst Avenue
    +1 323 663 0088
    carolyoung.com

04 Vamp
    1951 Hillhurst Avenue
    +1 323 662 1150
    vampshoeshop.com

05 High-Fidelity
    1956 Hillhurst Avenue
    +1 323 662 2000
    highfidelityla.com

06 Jeni's
    1954 Hillhurst Avenue
    +1 323 928 2668
    jenis.com

07 Vista Theater
    4473 Sunset Drive
    +1 323 660 6639
    vintagecinemas.com

08 Soap Plant & Wacko
    4633 Hollywood Boulevard
    +1 323 663 0122
    soapplant.com

09 The Dresden Restaurant
    1760 North
    Vermont Avenue
    +1 323 665 4294
    thedresden.com

10 Belljar
    1764 North
    Vermont Avenue
    +1 323 407 6446
    shop-belljar.com

11 The Arts Annex
    1814 North
    Vermont Avenue
    +1 323 660 1175
    skylightbooks.com

12 Bru Coffeebar
    1866 North
    Vermont Avenue
    +1 323 664 7500
    brucoffeebar.com

NEIGHBOURHOOD 03
Arts District
Blank canvas

Downtown LA is experiencing a renaissance led by the Arts District in the east. Bound by 1st Street, 7th Street, Alameda Street and the LA River, this pedestrian-friendly artists' community turned dining and retail destination just south of Little Tokyo is one to keep an eye on.

Gritty 20th-century warehouses and factories line the roads – some are still in use, others stand abandoned but most have been turned into studios, galleries, craft breweries, coffee roasters and shops. What was once the turf of artists such as Paul McCarthy and sculpturist Coleen Sterritt has become the home of contemporary craftsmen and creatives.

With the regeneration of the community has come a host of high-profile art galleries that have opened up here and just beyond the LA River in Boyle Heights. The most prominent is Hauser Wirth & Schimmel, an international gallery that moved into a restored Globe Mills factory, maintaining some of the street art that embellished its walls. Indeed, the Arts District has been a canvas for street artists such as ROA and Kim West for years.

With everything that's happening (including the construction of Michael Maltzan's new bridge, designed to replace the 6th Street Bridge across the river), this neighbourhood is changing fast. New places pop up and vanish every week; get there quick.

State of the art
Arts District walk

Kick off with a cup of cold brew from **1** *Blue Bottle Coffee* just around the corner from Willow Studios; bustling film crews can often be seen here caffeinating. Turn right down Mateo Street as you leave the coffee shop and follow it until you reach Palmetto Street. Here you'll find the all-white façade of **2** *Mama Gallery*, founded by Adarsha Benjamin and Eli Consilvio in 2014 to showcase contemporary artists ranging from LA-based Mattea Perrotta to Cole Sternberg.

Once you've toured the exhibition space you might want to pop in to **3** *The Factory Kitchen* for a meal. It's behind the gallery so wind your way from Palmetto Street to Alameda and onto Factory Place. As the name suggests this northern Italian trattoria run by chef Angelo Auriana and Matteo Ferdinandi is housed in an old factory loading dock, refurbished by Ana Henton of Mass Architecture & Design. After lunch retrace your steps to Palmetto Street and turn left onto Colyton, where you'll come across the **4** *Arts District Co-op*. It identifies itself as an "avant-garde market" and has plenty of independent brands to browse.

For a spot of culture head to the corner of Colyton and East 4th Street to the **5** *A+D Museum*, which opened here in 2015. It's the only museum in the city devoted to architecture exhibitions year-round and features projects by the likes of William F Cody and Ray Kappe as well as joint shows tackling big ideas such

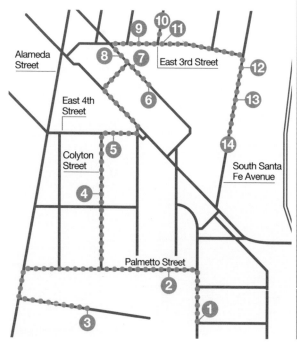

Address book

01 Blue Bottle Coffee
582 Mateo Street
bluebottlecoffee.com

02 Mama Gallery
1242 Palmetto Street
+1 213 256 0036
mama.gallery

03 The Factory Kitchen
1300 Factory Place
+1 213 996 6000
thefactorykitchen.com

04 Arts District Co-op
453 Colyton Street
+1 213 223 6717
adcoopla.com

05 A+D Museum
900 East 4th Street
+1 213 346 9734
aplusd.org

06 Arts District Brewing
Company
828 Traction Avenue
+1 213 519 5887
artsdistrictbrewing.com

07 The Box Gallery
805 Traction Avenue
+1 213 625 1747
theboxla.com

08 The Pie Hole
714 Traction Avenue
+1 213 537 0115
thepieholela.com

09 Apolis: Common Gallery
806 East 3rd Street
+1 213 613 9626
apolisglobal.com

10 Woo
209 South Garey Street
+1 213 687 4800
ilovewoo.com

11 Hauser Wirth & Schimmel
901 East 3rd Street
+1 213 943 1620
hauserwirthschimmel.com

12 Hue
300 South Santa Fe Avenue
+1 213 785 1191
placehue.com

13 The Voyager Shop
300 South Santa Fe Avenue
+1 213 995 9951
thevoyagershop.com

14 Westbound
300 South Santa Fe Avenue
+1 213 262 9291
westbounddtla.com

Getting there:

LA's rail network doesn't yet extend to the Arts District so your best bet is to drive to your destination and find parking where you can – try your luck in the Palmetto Lot at 1250 Palmetto Street. A less stressful option might be to hop on your bike.

as *Shelter: Rethinking How We Live in Los Angeles*.

By now you'll have earned yourself a pint of something cold so head right down East 4th Street then bear left around the corner up East 4th Place. Cut right down Hewitt Street and to your right, down Traction Avenue, you'll find the ❻ *Arts District Brewing Company*, where you can enjoy the potent Traction IPA and a game of ping pong.

Just over the road to your left is ❼ *The Box Gallery*, a contemporary arts space showcasing artists such as Barbara T Smith and Naotaka Hiro. Carry on a few steps up the street to ❽ *The Pie Hole* for a sneaky apple crumble or slice of Earl Grey-tea pie.

❾ *Apolis: Common Gallery*, an ethical LA men's and womenswear brand and gallery is just round the corner to the right on East 3rd Street. Turn right as you exit and then left onto South Garey Street to visit ❿ *Woo*, a fashion label founded by Staci Woo, who still makes all her designs by hand in the workshop at the back of the store.

Turn back to East 3rd Steet to find the impressive art complex ⓫ *Hauser Wirth & Schimmel*. Swiss couple Manuela and Iwan Wirth opened this branch to display the works of artists including Maria Lassnig, Isa Genzken and Hans Arp. There's also an on-site restaurant and curated public programmes.

Turn left as you leave, walk to the end of the street, then turn right onto South Santa Fe Avenue. Here you'll find boutiques galore; choose from ⓬ *Hue*, which carries brands such as Derek Lam, MSGM and Thakoon, or ⓭ *The Voyager Shop*, which collates clothing, homewares and accessories, including perfumes from Blackbird, soaps from Midnight Collective and denim jeans from THVM Atelier just around the corner.

After all that you'll need a sit down. Head a little further onto ⓮ *Westbound* and order their La Remedia house cocktail: Beefeater Gin, watermelon, grapefruit, lemon, lime, pink peppercorn and sea salt, all served in a highball with candied peppercorn. Cheers.

NEIGHBOURHOOD 04
Pasadena
Historic haunt

Part of Los Angeles County – and a city in its own right – Pasadena is a love letter to its past and home to an impressive collection of historic buildings. Old Town has some of the finest testaments to the golden age of the 1920s when revival architecture was at its peak; the Palladio-inspired Pasadena City Hall is one of the most beautiful in the west if not the country.

It started as a sleepy agricultural community before developing rapidly at the end of the 19th century. It was in this growth spurt that sewers, pavements and all the trappings of a modern city were built. In 1890 the first civic celebration of its kind was initiated at the Valley Hunt Club, a winter festivity involving horses decorated with flowers. Today that festival – the renowned Tournament of Roses – is still going strong.

Up to the 1930s construction was still rife, as evidenced by the plethora of Arts & Crafts structures in what is now the Bungalow Heaven neighbourhood (*see page 119*) and edifices such as the Rose Bowl stadium and Pasadena Playhouse. The Second World War put a stop to the growth and a period of decline ensued, marked by urban blight and gang problems.

Today Pasadena is back to its best thanks to the city's revitalisation programmes and it makes for a tranquil, history-steeped spot to walk around.

Standing pretty
Pasadena walk

Kick off this walk on Garfield Avenue facing ❶ *City Hall*. Completed in 1927 and marked by a central tower, the building dominates Pasadena's old town. Then turn left and walk to East Walnut Street for another impressive building, the ❷ *Pasadena Public Library*. An excellent example of Spanish colonial revival design, it was built in the same year as city hall by Myron Hunt and HC Chambers and is on the National Register of Historic Places. Pop in for a look at the impressive wood panelling.

As you come out of the library turn right down East Walnut Street to get to ❸ *Marston's*. Operating out of a Craftsman-style cottage, it's a slice of Americana (complete with a Star Spangled Banner) that happens to provide a good breakfast too. Refuel then head past the little park across the road to the ❹ *Levitt Pavilion Pasadena*. Dating back to 1930, it regularly hosts concerts, many of them for free.

A left on North Raymond Avenue brings you to the ❺ *Armory Center for the Arts* on the right. Part education centre, part exhibition space, it holds about 400 classes a year and has a host of Cali artists on display.

Once you've perused the centre, walk south. It may be time for a sushi lunch at ❻ *Osawa* on North Raymond Avenue on the next block. Opposite, reached by stairs from a brick courtyard, is ❼ *Vertical Wine Bistro*, which has a selection of Californian and

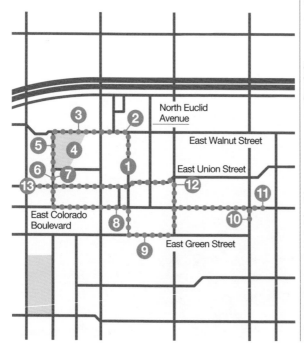

North Euclid Avenue

East Walnut Street

East Union Street

East Colorado Boulevard

East Green Street

European wines – perfect if you're after a sharpener.

Continue south down North Raymond Avenue to East Colorado Boulevard then turn left. Walk for three blocks and you'll come to ❽ *Plaza Pasadena Post Office* on the corner with Garfield. This building is best viewed from inside: constructed in the 1920s, it still boasts stunning detailing and a truly gorgeous stained-glass roof.

Once you've had a good look turn onto the Paseo Colorado pedestrianised area where you'll be able to spy the ❾ *Pasadena Civic Auditorium*, with its beautiful tiled frontage. Built in 1932, it was the home of the Emmy Awards for more than two decades and once a stop for shows touring the Broadway circuit.

Head back to East Colorado Boulevard and turn right. You'll pass the First United Methodist Church on the corner of South Oakland Avenue and just beyond it a great Spanish colonial revival building now inhabited by, ahem, Patioworld. Keep going until El Molino Avenue then take a right

to reach ❿ *The Pasadena Playhouse*. Another Spanish colonial revival building from 1924, it was home to the Gilmore Brown Players and to the College of Theater Arts, which produced actor Dustin Hoffman, among others.

From here head back to East Colorado Boulevard and turn right: on the left – if you can get past the horrible signage and building – is ⓫ *Vroman's Bookstore* that stocks arts and photography tomes. Dash back the way you came and turn right on North Los Robles Avenue. Here you'll spot the magnificent pagoda-like ⓬ *USC Pacific Asia Museum*, again from the 1920s. It's home to more than 15,000 objects celebrating the cultures of Asia and the Pacific Islands and worth a visit if you have time.

After all that you may need to rest your legs. Luckily your last stop is the excellent Italian-inspired ⓭ *Union* restaurant. Reach it by heading past the museum to East Union Street, turning left and walking just past the intersection with North Raymond Avenue.

Getting there

The Gold Line of the Metro light rail connects Pasadena with Downtown LA (change to the Gold Line at Union Station). Head towards APU/Citrus College and get off at the Memorial Park stop; alternatively Del Mar and Lake are also walking distance from the city hall.

Address book

01 City Hall
100 Garfield Avenue
+1 626 744 4000
ci.pasadena.ca.us

02 Pasadena Public Library
285 East Walnut Street
+1 626 744 4066
ci.pasadena.ca.us/library

03 Marston's
151 East Walnut Street
+1 626 796 2459
marstonsrestaurant.com

04 Levitt Pavilion Pasadena
Memorial Park
85 East Holly Street
+1 626 683 3230
levittpavilionpasadena.org

05 Armory Center for the Arts
145 North Raymond Avenue
+1 626 792 5101
armoryarts.org

06 Osawa
77 North Raymond Avenue
+1 626 683 1150
theosawa.com

07 Vertical Wine Bistro
70 North Raymond Avenue
+1 626 795 3999
verticalwinebistro.com

08 Plaza Pasadena Post Office
281 East Colorado Boulevard
+1 626 744 0212

09 Pasadena Civic Auditorium
300 East Green Street
+1 626 795 9311
pasadenacivic.visitpasadena.com

10 The Pasadena Playhouse
39 South El Molino Avenue
+1 626 356 7529
pasadenaplayhouse.org

11 Vroman's Bookstore
695 East Colorado Boulevard
+1 626 449 5320
vromansbookstore.com

12 USC Pacific Asia Museum
46 North Los Robles Avenue
+1 626 449 2742
pacificasiamuseum.org

13 Union
37 East Union Street
+1 626 795 5841
unionpasadena.com

NEIGHBOURHOOD 05
Venice
Water under the bridge

Inspired by its grand Italian namesake, Venice was designed
as a seaside resort in 1904. The man with the plan was tobacco
tycoon Abbot Kinney, who secured the one-and-a-half-mile
stretch of then "worthless" marshland in LA's property boom
in the late 1800s. Engineers advised him to dig canals to reclaim
the land, which was bordered by the Pacific coast to the west,
Marina del Rey to the south, Mar Vista to the east and Santa
Monica to the north.

Three years later Kinney had created a complete network
of canals linked to the ocean, criss-crossed by bridges and
traversed by gondolas. On 4 July 1905 The US's Little Venice
officially opened, complete with amusement pier. It swiftly
became the most popular destination on the Pacific Electric
streetcar line and was dubbed the Coney Island of the Pacific.
But by 1912 the canals were declared a health risk and today
only a small section remains.

By the time Los Angeles annexed the independent city in
1925 its grandeur had faded. It wasn't until 1982 that Venice's
cultural value was acknowledged and it was made a Historic
District. Today it's a holiday town once more and entertainment
is the name of the game.

Canalside cruise
Venice walk

Start your saunter through
Venice at the ❶ *Rose Café* on
Rose Avenue; the freshly-baked
pastries and chef Jason Neroni's
breakfast burrito will make it more
than worth your while.

Once your appetite has been
sated turn left and round the
corner onto Main Street. Marvel
at Frank Gehry's sculptural
❷ *Binoculars Building*, (Google's
LA office), before hanging a left
down Sunset Avenue. Turn right
on Hampton Drive before taking
another right down Brooks Avenue
until you hit the famed Abbot
Kinney Boulevard, named after the
neighbourhood's founder. Follow
it left and begin your window-
shopping spree at ❸ *Cuyana*, a
San Francisco-based womenswear
brand established by Karla
Gallardo and Shilpa Shah, known
for their personalised leather
accessories. A little further down
on your right is Scandinavian
enclave ❹ *Huset*, its walls lined
with ceramic mugs by Mette
Duedahl, Menu planters and
Swedish chairs.

Seldom is coffee served
as meticulously as it is at
❺ *Intelligentsia Coffee* just across
the road. Fired up on a creamy
cup of whole-bean brew, cross
the street to explore the unique
craftshop ❻ *Chariots on Fire*
before picking up some novelties
and cards at ❼ *Burro* on the
left-hand side of the street.

Had enough walking? Lie
down and be pampered at the
❽ *Caudalie Boutique Spa*; we'd
recommend the Divine Body

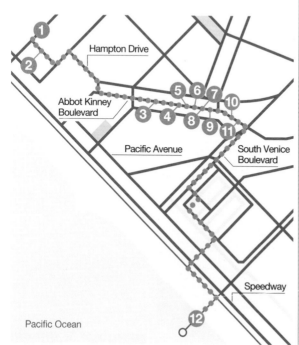

Hampton Drive

Abbot Kinney
Boulevard

Pacific Avenue

South Venice
Boulevard

Speedway

Pacific Ocean

Address book

01   Rose Café
220 Rose Avenue
+1 310 399 0711
rosecafevenice.com

02   Binoculars Building
340 Main Street

03   Cuyana
1140 Abbot Kinney
Boulevard
+1 310 450 7239
cuyana.com

04   Huset
1316 Abbot Kinney
Boulevard
+1 424 268 4213
huset-shop.com

05   Intelligentsia Coffee
1331 Abbot Kinney
Boulevard
+1 310 399 1233
intelligentsiacoffee.com

06   Chariots on Fire
1342 1/2 Abbot Kinney
Boulevard
+1 310 450 3088
chariotsonfire.com

07   Burro
1409 Abbot Kinney
Boulevard
+1 310 450 6288
burrogoods.com

08   Caudalie Boutique Spa
1416 Abbot Kinney
Boulevard
+1 310 450 3560
us.caudalie.com

9   Gjelina Take Away
1427 Abbot Kinney
Boulevard
+1 310 392 7575
gjelinatakeaway.com

10   The Tasting Kitchen
1633 Abbot Kinney
Boulevard
+1 310 392 6644
thetastingkitchen.com

11   Ilan Dei Venice
1650 Abbot Kinney
Boulevard
+1 310 729 2713
ilandeivenice.com

12   Venice Fishing Pier
Venice Beach

Treatment massage. Next on the agenda is lunch: try a slice of pizza topped with burrata and cherry tomatoes from Travis Lett's ⑨ *Gjelina Take Away* (the deli version of the sit-down restaurant of the same name next door) or enjoy a more substantial meal by renowned chef Casey Lane at ⑩ *The Tasting Kitchen*.

Once you've had your fill (and perhaps a cheeky scoop of ice cream from Salt & Straw) there's time for one more stop before tackling the historic canals. ⑪ *Ilan Dei Venice* is uniquely Californian (not many places boast weather so consistently favourable to allow for open-air shopping) and sells everything from jewellery to garden furniture.

Follow the street until you reach the main intersection. Cross to the other side and head down South Venice Boulevard until Dell Avenue: turn left and you'll soon be at the canals of Venice. It may be hard to believe but this is what a large portion of the neighbourhood once looked like. Cross the first canal and turn right onto Carroll

Canal Walk. Follow the path around the corner along the Grand Canal. Weave your way over three historic white-painted wooden bridges until you reach the fourth canal. Cross over the last bridge onto the far side of the Grand Canal.

Follow the pathway over Strongs Drive and then Pacific Avenue on narrow 27th Avenue until you reach the beach promenade. This section of a 35km-long bike trail known as The Strand runs along the Pacific shoreline from Will Rogers State Beach in Pacific Palisades to Torrance Beach in the south. Follow the trail heading left towards the ⑫ *Venice Fishing Pier*.

Watch the surfers show off their moves as you wander down the boardwalk but mind the rods and buckets left behind by fishermen waiting for their big catch. Take in the view (you can see all the way up to Santa Monica Pier), then meander back along the sandy shore to your start point.

Getting there
——
We'd recommend driving (or even better, being driven) to Venice. There's a Minuteman parking lot at 512 Rose Avenue. Alternatively jump on the Metro Rapid Line 733 to Venice & Lincoln, or Metro lines 333 and 33, which both go to Venice Beach from Union Station.

Resources
—— Inside knowledge

Los Angeles can be challenging for visitors so you're going to need all of the information on these pages to help you navigate it in style (while whistling one of the city's seminal tunes, of course). Public transport hasn't traditionally been the city's strong point but this is slowly changing, despite Angelenos' reliance on the automobile. Whatever your mode of transport, it's time to plan your itinerary: the following lists of top events and all-weather activities will help. We've also thrown in a bit of local lingo for good measure.

Transport
Get around town

01 **Metro:** The city's Metro service (four light rails, two subways and buses) is not as bad as you might think. The Downtown to Santa Monica light rail (Metro Expo line expansion) is slow but it still beats rush-hour traffic. While buses still accept cash, most trains don't: purchase a TAP card at a station. Single trips cost $1.75; a day pass is $7. *metro.net*

02 **Car:** Consider renting at the airport. There are plenty of car parks and most venues offer valet parking. For private car hire, LA Confidential and A&E Worldwide are reliable. *la-confidential.us aeworldwidelimo.com*

03 **Bike:** There are a number of public bike-share schemes operating in various districts. Metro Bike Share is Downtown's and costs $3.50 for the initial 30 minutes. Santa Monica's system, Breeze, has pick-up points on Rose Avenue to Ocean Front Walk in Venice. West Hollywood has a brand new network of hubs called WeHo Pedals. *bikeshare.metro.net santamonicabikeshare.com wehopedals.com*

04 **On foot:** Venice and Santa Monica are "ped" friendly, as are parts of Hollywood such as Los Feliz. Downtown can be walked but be careful about straying into Skid Row.

05 **Taxi:** Taxis can be hired across the city but app-based car services are more reliable and cheaper. City services include Yellow Cab and City Cab. *taxicabsla.org*

06 **Flights:** LAX lies 20km away from Downtown. Bob Hope Airport services West Coast destinations; Long Beach Airport runs some national routes. Always allow extra travel time for traffic jams. *lawa.org lgb.org bobhopeairport.com*

Vocabulary
Local lingo

01 **Animal style:** a "secret" menu style at burger chain In-N-Out that involves a patty fried in mustard
02 **CPT:** Compton
03 **Dank:** really good, excellent
04 **Doing background:** working as an extra in a film
05 **May grey/June gloom:** the foggy mornings common in late spring and early summer
06 **PCH:** Pacific Coast Highway
07 **SoCal:** Southern California
08 **The Strand:** popular name for the Marvin Braude Bike Trail running along the beach
09 **The Valley:** San Fernando Valley

Soundtrack to the city
Five top tunes

01 **The Mamas & The Papas, 'California Dreamin':** A 1966 belter from one of the greatest bands to ever come out of the US. Contains the lyric: "I'd be safe and warm, if I was in LA".
02 **Guns N' Roses, 'Welcome to the Jungle':** Axl Rose's soaring falsetto is employed to the max in this 1987 hit. The song looks at LA's dark underbelly and the people who flock there in search of fame and fortune.
03 **BB King, 'Back in LA':** The blues legend's homage to the city is a spine-tingler from the 1991 album *There Is Always One More Time*.
04 **Billy Joel, 'Los Angelenos':** This timeless take on the allure of LA was released on the Piano Man's 1974 album *Streetlife Serenade*.
05 **Weezer, 'Beverly Hills':** A tongue-in-cheek look at life in Beverly Hills from 2005 by the homegrown indie rock band: "Look at all those movie stars, they're all so beautiful and clean."

Best events
What to see

01 **Golden Globe Awards, Beverly Hills:** The Tinseltown year kicks off with this annual Hollywood love-in, rewarding film and TV talent.
January, goldenglobes.com

02 **LA Art Show, Downtown:** This three-decades strong celebration of the visual arts, with a focus on modern and contemporary, welcomes about 70,000 punters.
January, laartshow.com

03 **Academy Awards, Hollywood:** The night when the city's A-list actors don their glad rags to cry and laugh along with fellow luvvies.
February, oscar.go.com

04 **Grammy Awards, Downtown:** What the Oscars are to film, the Grammys are to music.
February, grammy.com

05 **LA Marathon, Downtown to Santa Monica:** This spring race is one of the largest marathons in the US. There's a range of events held in the week around it.
March, lamarathon.com

06 **Coachella, Indio:** The US's best and most popular music festival is held 200km out of town in the Colorado Desert.
April, coachella.com

07 **Noho Theatre & Arts Festival, North Hollywood:** One of the region's longest-running arts celebrations, with theatre, music, art, dance and food.
May, nohoartsdistrict.com

08 **LA Film Festival, Culver City:** Hosted by Film Independent, this event celebrates indie film, world cinema and documentaries.
June, filmindependent.org

09 **LA Fashion Week, various venues:** This is one of the biggest events on the US fashion calendar.
October, lafw.net

10 **LA Auto Show, Downtown:** A celebration of cars in a city that's addicted to them.
November, laautoshow.com

Sunny day
The great outdoors

With low rainfall and a balmy Mediterranean climate, Los Angeles is a city built for spending time outdoors. Here's what not to miss.

01 **Beach time:** The sun is out and there's no better way to enjoy the rays than by heading to the coast. You could go to either Venice or Santa Monica beach – probably the closest and both fascinating for people watching – but we recommend heading to Malibu, a little further down the coast. Check out the stunning Point Dume State Beach or hire a board and a wetsuit and pretend to be a Californian at Surfrider Beach.
parks.ca.gov

02 **Desert calling:** Take the two-hour trip out to Joshua Tree National Park and experience the dry-as-a-bone scrubland that feels a million miles away from the metropolis. Stay the night to experience the stars and make sure you call in at the bizarre Pioneertown (built as a movie set in the 1940s) and eat at Pappy & Harriet's.
pappyandharriets.com

03 **Go for a hike:** Los Angeles may be rightly known for its terrible traffic jams and lung-blackening smog, yet it also never fails to delight with its natural wonders. Being able to go on a proper hike here is one of the city's great joys. Lace up those boots and check out Runyon Canyon (see page 126), Griffith Park (see page 126) or Temescal Gateway Park (see page 127).
nps.gov

Rainy day
Weather-proof activities

It's unusual for the weather to put a dampener on proceedings, but should the situation arise we've got you covered.

01 **Catch a movie:** You're in the film capital of the world, so what could be a more fitting way to deal with the drizzle than by taking in a flick at one of LA's many historic cinemas? Read our Culture section for options (see page 102 – 104) but some recommendations include the quirky Vista in Los Feliz or ArcLight Cinema's restored Cinerama Dome that dates back to 1963.
vintagecinemas.com/vista
arclightcinemas.com

02 **Drink and graze:** Los Angeles has some excellent food halls where you can sample from the entire multicultural spectrum of cuisines. If you're Downtown Grand Central Market (see page 44) is a must. Also worth a gander is El Mercado de Los Angeles (otherwise known as El Mercadito), a fascinating, slightly kitsch window on the city's Latino soul, and the historic (but poorly named) Original Farmers Market in Fairfax. There are also many and varied outdoor farmers markets that pop up on weekends from Santa Monica to Pasadena.
grandcentralmarket.com
farmersmarketla.com

03 **The Broad, Downtown:** This museum recently opened inside a mega-statement $140m building (see page 93). It hosts some 2,000 works of art from the collection of philanthropists Eli and Edythe Broad.
thebroad.org

About Monocle
—— Step inside

In 2007, Monocle was launched as a monthly magazine briefing on global affairs, business, culture, design and much more. We believed there was a globally minded audience of readers who were hungry for opportunities and experiences beyond their national borders.

Today Monocle is a complete media brand with print, audio and online elements – not to mention our expanding network of shops and cafés. Besides our London HQ we have seven international bureaux in New York, Toronto, Istanbul, Singapore, Tokyo, Zürich and Hong Kong. We continue to grow and flourish and at our core is the simple belief that there will always be a place for a print brand that is committed to telling fresh stories and sending photographers on assignments. It's also a case of knowing that our success is all down to the readers, advertisers and collaborators who have supported us along the way.

Monocle menu
—
We have cafés in London and Tokyo

❶

Retail and cafés
Food for thought

Via our shops in Hong Kong, Toronto, New York, Tokyo, London and Singapore we sell products that cater to our readers' tastes and are produced in collaboration with brands we believe in. We also have cafés in Tokyo and London. And if you are in the UK capital, visit the Kioskafé in Paddington, which combines good coffee and great reads.

❷

Online
Digital delivery

We have a dynamic website: *monocle.com*. As well as being the place to hear our radio station, Monocle 24, the site presents our films, which are beautifully shot and edited by our in-house team and provide a fresh perspective on our stories. Check out the films celebrating the cities that make up our Travel Guide Series before you explore the rest of the site.

❸

International bureaux
Boots on the ground

We have an HQ in London and call upon firsthand reports from our contributors in more than 35 cities around the world. We also have seven international bureaux; for this travel guide New York bureau chief Ed Stocker and deputy bureau chief Megan Billings teamed up with MONOCLE writer Marie-Sophie Schwarzer. They also called on the assistance of Los Angeles-based writers to ensure that we covered the best food, retail, hospitality and entertainment the city has to offer. The aim is to make you, the reader, feel like a local when you visit the City of Angels.

4
Radio
Sound approach

Monocle 24 is our round-the-clock
radio station that was launched in
2011. It delivers global news and
shows covering foreign affairs,
urbanism, business, culture, food
and drink, design and print media.
When you find yourself in Los
Angeles, tune into *The Daily* to
hear regular reports from our
Toronto and New York bureaus
and interviews with guests from
across the Americas region. We also
have a playlist to accompany you
day and night, regularly assisted by
live band sessions that are hosted at
our headquarters. You can listen
to our shows live or download
them from *monocle.com*, iTunes
or SoundCloud.

5
Print
Committed to the page

MONOCLE is published 10 times
a year. We have stayed loyal to our
belief in quality print with two extra
seasonal publications: THE FORECAST,
packed with key insights into the
year ahead, and THE ESCAPIST, our
summer travel-minded magazine.
To sign up visit *monocle.com/
subscribe*. Since 2013 we have also
been publishing books, like this one,
in partnership with Gestalten.

Join the club

01
Subscribe to Monocle
A subscription is a simple
way to make sure you never
miss a copy and enjoy many
additional benefits.

02
Read every issue published
Our subscribers have
exclusive access to the entire
Monocle archive, and have
priority access to selected
product collaborations at
monocle.com.

03
Never miss an issue
Subscription copies are
delivered to your door no
matter where you are in
the world and we offer
an auto-renewal service
to ensure that you never
miss an issue.

04
And there's more...
Subscribers benefit from a
10 per cent discount at all
Monocle shops, including
online, and receive exclusive
offers and invitations to
events around the world.

**Choose your
package**

Premium one year
12 × issues
+ Porter Sub Club bag

One year
12 × issues
+ Monocle Voyage tote bag

Six months
6 × issues

Chief photographer
Ye Rin Mok

Still life
David Sykes

Images
Yasmin Alishav
Mike Beiriger
Chris Burden
Brianne Chan
Alicia Cho
Lauren Coleman
Eames Foundation
Kenji Fitzgerald
Kim Garcia
Adrian Gaut
Getty Images
Go Get Em Tiger
Art Gray
David Hartwell
Andy J Scott
Dylan + Jeni
Amanda Kho
Emily Knecht
Nikolas Koenig
Kristine Lefebvre
Los Angeles Philharmonic
Association
Spencer Lowell
Johnston Marklee
Chateau Marmont
James Martinez
Michael Maltzan Architecture
Ryan Miller
Norton Simon Art Foundation
Paul + Williams
Sisilia Piring
Rick Poon
Sierra Prescott
Elon Schoenholz
Zen Sekizawa
Skandia Shafer
Surfing Cowboys
Josh Telles
Ken Tisuthiwongse
Alex Vertikoff
Joshua White
Eric Wolfinger
Bert Youn
Federico Zignani

Illustrators
Satoshi Hashimoto
Ceylan Sahin
Tokuma

Writers
Megan Billings
Robert Bound
Melkon Charchoglyan
Dennis Evanosky
Josh Fehnert
Edward Lawrenson
Kurt Lin
Nathan Masters
Charlie Monaghan
Melissa Richardson Banks
Ben Rylan
Marie-Sophie Schwarzer
Ed Stocker
Lily Stockman
Steve Van Doren
Josh Welsh
Julia Wick
Joy Yoon

Monocle
EDITOR IN CHIEF AND CHAIRMAN
Tyler Brûlé
EDITOR
Andrew Tuck
CREATIVE DIRECTOR
Richard Spencer Powell

**The Monocle Travel Guide
Series: Los Angeles**
GUIDE EDITOR
Ed Stocker
ASSOCIATE EDITORS
Megan Billings
Marie-Sophie Schwarzer
PHOTO EDITOR
Faye Sakura Rentoule

**The Monocle Travel Guide
Series**
SERIES EDITOR
Joe Pickard
ASSOCIATE EDITOR, BOOKS
Amy Richardson
RESEARCHER/WRITER
Mikaela Aitken
DESIGNERS
Jay Yeo
Sam Brogan
PHOTO EDITORS
Matthew Beaman
Faye Sakura Rentoule
Shin Miura

PRODUCTION
Jacqueline Deacon
Dan Poole
Chloë Ashby
Sean McGeady
Sonia Zhuravlyova

CHAPTER EDITING

Need to know
Ed Stocker

Hotels
Megan Billings

Food and drink
Megan Billings

Retail
Megan Billings

Things we'd buy
Megan Billings

Essays
Ed Stocker

Culture
Marie-Sophie Schwarzer

Design and architecture
Ed Stocker

Sport and fitness
Marie-Sophie Schwarzer

Walks
Ed Stocker

Resources
Ed Stocker

Research
Mikaela Aitken
Pete Kempshall
Aidan McLaughlin
Ximena Miñan Vega
Clarissa Pharr
Kerala Woods
Zayana Zulkiflee

Special thanks
Andrea Alonso
*Louise Bourgeois/The Eastern
Foundation*
Eitan Braham
Anthony Carfello
Lucia Dewey Atwood
Adrian Fine
Susan Garbett
Douglas Geller
Joshua Herman
Rachel Krupa
Edward Lawrenson
Pete van Leeuwen
Joy Limanon
Sarah Lorenzen
Dashiell Manley
Anita Maritz
Anne McCaddon
Tina Miller
John Ripley
Sheryl Scott
Robert Stark
Gillian Sturtevant
Geoff Thompson
Tracy Wilkinson
Paul Witt

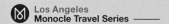

New

The collection

We hope you have found the Monocle Travel Guide to Los Angeles useful, inspiring and entertaining. There's plenty more to get your teeth into: we have a global suite of guides with many more set to be released in coming months. Cities are fun. Let's explore.

❶ London

The sights, sounds and style

❷ New York

Get a taste for the Big Apple's best

❸ Tokyo

The enigmatic glory of Japan's capital

❹ Hong Kong

Down to business in this vibrant city

❺ Madrid

Captivating capital abuzz with spirit

❻ Bangkok

Stimulate your senses with the exotic

❼ Istanbul

Thrilling fusion of Asia and Europe

❽ Miami

Unpack the Magic City's box of tricks

❾ Rio de Janeiro

Beaches, bars and bossa nova

❿ Paris

Be romanced by the City of Light

⓫ Singapore

Where modernity meets tradition

⓬ Vienna

Waltz through the Austrian capital

⓭ Sydney

Sun, surf and urban delights

⓮ Honolulu

Embrace Hawaii's aloha spirit

⓯ Copenhagen

Cycle through the Danish capital

⓰ Los Angeles

Fly high in the City of Angels

THE TEMPLE COVENANT

(The Temple - Book 3)

This third novel in The Temple series follows young church minister Helen Johnson and archaeologist Sam Cameron as their quiet sabbatical break in East Africa explodes into a wild and deadly chase across international borders, through cities and into the unforgiving bush. The Templar mystery continues as new enemies emerge.

30130 5061 6206 3